CultureShock!
A Survival Guide to Customs and Etiquette

Bulgaria

Agnes Sachsenroeder

mc Marshall Cavendish
Editions

This 2nd edition published in 2011 by:
Marshall Cavendish Corporation
99 White Plains Road
Tarrytown, NY 10591-9001
www.marshallcavendish.us

Other Marshall Cavendish Offices:
Marshall Cavendish International (Asia) Private Limited. 1 New Industrial Road,
Singapore 536196 ■ Marshall Cavendish International. PO Box 65829, London
EC1P 1NY, UK ■ Marshall Cavendish International (Thailand) Co Ltd. 253 Asoke,
12th Flr, Sukhumvit 21 Road, Klongtoey Nua, Wattana, Bangkok 10110, Thailand
■ Marshall Cavendish (Malaysia) Sdn Bhd, Times Subang, Lot 46, Subang Hi-Tech
Industrial Park, Batu Tiga, 40000 Shah Alam, Selangor Darul Ehsan, Malaysia

Marshall Cavendish is a trademark of Times Publishing Limited

IISBN 13: 978-0-7614-5877-7

Please contact the publisher for the Library of Congress catalog number

Printed in Singapore by Times Printers Pte Ltd

Photo Credits:
All black and white photos by the author. All colour photos from
Photolibrary except page h (Getty Images). ■ Cover photo: Photolibrary

All illustrations by TRIGG

ABOUT THE SERIES

Culture shock is a state of disorientation that can come over anyone who has been thrust into unknown surroundings, away from one's comfort zone. *CultureShock!* is a series of trusted and reputed guides which has, for decades, been helping expatriates and long-term visitors to cushion the impact of culture shock whenever they move to a new country.

Written by people who have lived in the country and experienced culture shock themselves, the authors share all the information necessary for anyone to cope with these feelings of disorientation more effectively. The guides are written in a style that is easy to read and covers a range of topics that will arm readers with enough advice, hints and tips to make their lives as normal as possible again.

Each book is structured in the same manner. It begins with the first impressions that visitors will have of that city or country. To understand a culture, one must first understand the people—where they came from, who they are, the values and traditions they live by, as well as their customs and etiquette. This is covered in the first half of the book

Then on with the practical aspects—how to settle in with the greatest of ease. Authors walk readers through how to find accommodation, get the utilities and telecommunications up and running, enrol the children in school and keep in the pink of health. But that's not all. Once the essentials are out of the way, venture out and try the food, enjoy more of the culture and travel to other areas. Then be immersed in the language of the country before discovering more about the business side of things.

To round off, snippets of basic information are offered before readers are 'tested' on customs and etiquette of the country. Useful words and phrases, a comprehensive resource guide and list of books for further research are also included for easy reference.

CONTENTS

PREFACE

I have tried to make sure that the observations in this book are common denominators distilled from as many people´s opinions as possible, but ultimately they are still common denominators as I see them. We all see things differently and react in diverse ways to any one situation, so this book merely provides signposts, and each person will discover aspects of Bulgaria for himself/herself.

While every effort was made to keep the information the most up-to-date, Bulgaria is developing so quickly that between the time this book went to press and your reading it, some things, like phone numbers, websites and addresses, may have changed or new shops may have sprung up or even folded. So before you launch into any undertaking based on the information in this book, it´s a good idea to just double check again, in case you dash into a dental office only to find a sex shop in its place.

Happy exploring!

Grateful thanks to the many people, both Bulgarians and expatriates, who have obligingly answered my questions. Many of them were my unsuspecting neighbours at official dinners, who had to see their food turn cold as they patiently replied to my interrogations. In order to get spontaneous answers, I never divulged why I was asking all these relentless questions in between mouthfuls. I hope I didn´t spoil their enjoyment of the food too much.

I was also utterly relieved when I first arrived in Bulgaria to find that some excellent guides existed to help me navigate my way around my new host country. These are listed in the further reading section at the end of the book and I highly recommend them to all newcomers. The various news media and magazines I mentioned in this book also helped me significantly in my research.

I would not have lived in Bulgaria in the first place, if not for my husband´s job posting. The nature of his job also presented me the opportunity to meet with some interesting people and experience events which I otherwise would not have.

MAP OF BULGARIA

FIRST IMPRESSIONS

CHAPTER 1

'All that we know is still infinitely less than
all that remains unknown.'
—William Harvey, English physician

MY FIRST IMPRESSION

I entered Bulgaria, not through Sofia International Airport, but across the Romanian-Bulgarian border by car. Having heard about the corruption at immigration checkpoints, I wondered what my husband and I might face, since we looked like gypsies with a car bursting at the seams with personal belongings.

`No payment required here´ read the signs at immigration check-points on both sides of the border, in a multitude of languages. We were impressed. We encountered no problems. Perhaps the impending accession into the European Union had something to do with it.

The only unusual thing which happened was our having to drive through a shallow pool to disinfect our tyres from whatever Romanian infections. We were not required to be hosed down; I was most relieved, but wondered about the bacteria clinging to us and our belongings in the car. We drove over the (not quite blue) Danube, as it acts as a natural border between Romania and Bulgaria. I was wondering before that if the recent severe floodings would cause problems, but the bridge was way above the swollen river. A magnificent view it was, looking down at the swirling, angry river. Exactly at the mid-point of the bridge was a sign that welcomed us into Bulgaria. We had entered the country of our next posting.

Had I fallen asleep crossing the border, I would still know I was in Bulgaria the minute I opened my eyes. All the signs were in Cyrillic. I had been frantically trying to learn the Cyrillic alphabet in the past weeks, and tried to see if I could read the signs. By the time I figured out the first two letters, we were a kilometre down the road. Then I saw one which I could read—'PYCE'. Hurray. No wait, it wasn't Pyce as in English, but 'RUSE', the name of the city on the Danube we had just passed. 'P' in Cyrillic is 'R' in Latin, 'Y' is 'U' and 'C' is 'S'. But 'E' is also 'E'. Sigh. I knew I had my work cut out for me in Bulgaria.

I consoled myself that I would learn the Cyrillic alphabet in good time, and decided to take in the countryside instead. It was charmingly bucolic. Occasionally, donkey and horse-carts would travel on the narrow country roads, slowing traffic down to like in a funeral procession. Some Bulgarians who appeared to be failed Formula-One drivers got the frustration off their chests by overtaking at top speed, regardless of whether there were cars coming in the opposite direction or not.

Traditional horsedrawn carts share the roads with cars, even in the capital, Sofia.

We stopped at a restaurant for an input and output break. It still retained its socialist ambience, but had a good, strong espresso which perked us up. A visit to the toilet led me to take away two stars from the restaurant. It was extremely dark, and myopic me had trouble groping my way around. Entering the cubicle, I noticed the hole in the ground in time not to put my foot into it. Obviously squat toilets were still in use in the countryside.

The good thing about going into a new place by starting from outside the city is that the infrastructure only gets better. The roads improved as we neared Sofia, the capital. There were blocks of socialist-era flats but as we entered the city centre, we were met by imposing historical buildings standing among less inspiring ones. With no skycrapers, and hardly many buildings higher than eight stories, I could catch a glimpse of the silhouette of Mount Vitosha in the distance.

We inched our car along the jammed roads. A role reversal had taken place. The cars had become pedestrians and parked themselves smugly on the sidewalk, forcing the pedestrians to pose as cars and walk on the roads. We found our hotel without too much trouble, but couldn´t find a place

Views of mighty Mount Vitosha with its snow-capped peak can be seen from many parts of Sofia.

to park our car. In desperation, I hopped out and removed two pylons placed in front of the hotel on the pavement so that we could at least stop to unload our luggages.

We had opted to stay in a smaller hotel instead of one of those from an international chain. It was as four-star as it advertised itself to be—modern and cosy, with a good restaurant, and the staff were efficient.

As I got into bed that night, I had a feeling I would not have too much trouble settling into Sofia, once I got my Cyrillic alphabet in order.

Bulgaria might have been somewhat off most people´s radar screen some years back, but its international profile has increased after becoming a new kid on the block in the European Union (EU) family in January 2007.

For the average John, Claus, Emile and Erik of Western Europe, Bulgarians may be either a headache or a blessing. These new European cousins could mean welcomed cheap labour, or it could mean competition in the job market. Having experienced the influx of Eastern European workers into their countries when 10 new countries joined the EU in 2004, some Western Europeans were nervous that there would another wave of `Polish plumbers´ coming their way. Many governments felt the public concern, and dutifully imposed restrictions on Bulgarian and Romanian workers.

Juan, Joao, Luigi and Odysseus of the Mediterranean countries are a little more familiar with Bulgarians. Spain, Portugal, Italy and Greece already host a significant concentration of Bulgarian migrant workers even before 2007.

Those with a longer memory might remember Bulgaria for the notorious assassination of Bulgarian dissident, Georgi Markov, in London in 1978. Markov was dramatically killed by a dart (filled with the poison ricin) fired from an umbrella as he waited at a bus-stop. Shortly before that, there was an attempt to liquidate another Bulgarian dissident, Vladimir Kostov. Kostov was hit by a similar ricin pellet, but he owed his life to a thick sweater which prevented the pellet from penetrating fully into his body.

Others might be familiar with the more recent unfortunate case of five Bulgarian nurses and a Palestinian doctor (who

was given Bulgarian citizenship in June 2007) jailed in Libya since 1999 for allegedly infecting Libyan children with HIV. After eight agonising years and difficult negotiations between the EU and Libya, they were finally freed and returned to Bulgaria on July 24 2007.

People who have been following Bulgaria's accession into the European Union will remember words and phrases like corruption, money laundering and organised crime in the European Commission's monitoring reports. In the media, one reads about the more than 120 contract killings of gangsters, a former prime minister, businessmen, bankers and football club owners between 1996 and 2006, and right through 2007 (after the country became an EU member).

From all these, one might go away with the idea that Bulgaria is a natural film set for the next James Bond or Godfather movie. But it isn't. The average expatriate who lives and works legally in Bulgaria is not likely to come across a Bulgarian Don Corleone or any of his men-in-black with dark shades. With caution and luck, foreigners might not even encounter any of the usual crimes associated with cities—mugging, burglary and pickpocketing. And the umbrellas that Bulgarians have in their hands these days are genuinely for protection against the rain, not sinister killing weapons.

The Capital Sofia*

- Capital since 1879
- Named Serdica under the Romans
- Renamed Triaditsa by Byzantines, Sredets by Bulgars
- Renamed Sofia in 1376, after St. Sophia church
- Situated 550 m (2805 ft) above sea level
- Population: 1.2 million (2008 est)
- Tallest building: Rodina Hotel (104 m/341 ft)

*pronounced Sofiya, meaning wisdom in Greek

Bulgaria managed to free itself from communism only in 1990, so there are still socialist reminders in the country. According to the World Bank, its GDP per capita (purchasing power parity) estimated for 2009 is about US$ 12,600, putting it into the band of the poorer countries in Europe. But Bulgaria is not a decaying country in monotonous grey. On the contrary, it boasts magnificent mountain ranges with 12 National Parks. The socialist-era buildings are still there, but so are many historical monuments and archaeological sites. A real treat for history buffs. But those who prefer modern-day entertainment will be pleased to know that shopping malls, restaurants and bars and discos are mushrooming in the capital, Sofia, and major cities faster than you can say `Paris Hilton´.

Simon Anholt, a specialist in advising countries how to market themselves and author of *Competitive Identity*, has noted wryly that almost every country claims to be a crossroads or a gateway (or both) and presents itself as a `land of contrasts´. But Bulgaria can honestly make that claim with its location and its modern cities contrasted against unspoilt rustic villages and ancient sites; socialist symbols against capitalist ones; and pop culture competing with an intact wealth of traditions. Diversity is how the Bulgarian tourist industry likes to describe the country, and so it is.

How a foreigner finds Bulgaria will depend on his/her previous experiences. For those who have no experience of developing countries, they might feel some discomfort in the beginning, while those who have a clutch of `hardship postings´ under their belt may find Bulgaria a welcome relief. To a lesser extent, who you are (your nationality, your skin colour) may also affect the ease with which you settle into Bulgaria, but more on that later in Chapter 4.

What most foreigners find daunting (unless you´re Russian, Macedonian or a language genius) is grappling with a whole new alphabet—Cyrillic. Adjusting to a new country is made so much harder by not being able to read anything at all, not even the street names. But with determination and a swig of the national spirit, *rakia*, for courage, one will manage to pick it up, if only because you do want to know which street you´re standing on and what the stuff might be before imbibing.

With Bulgaria now in the European Union, more improvements are expected in the coming years. Coming to Bulgaria now will be markedly different from what your predecessors experienced only a few years ago.

So, *Dobre Doschli*! (Welcome!)

OVERVIEW

CHAPTER 2

'The proud old Balkan Range. Above the Danube blue,
The sun is bright on Thrace. It smiles on Pirin too.
Chorus:
O Motherland most dear, you, paradise on earth,
Your beauty, your glory are endless in their birth!'
—*Mila Rodino*, the Bulgarian National Anthem

THE MANY-FACETED LAND

Bulgaria is in Southeastern Europe, on the Balkan Peninsula, and to be more precise, it is located at 43'00 N and 25'00 E. That places it roughly about the same distance north of the Equator as Portland (Maine), Marseilles and Florence. Its northern neighbour is Romania, and Greece and Turkey are its southern neighbours. Bulgaria shares its western border with (the former Yugoslav states) of Macedonia, and Serbia and Montenegro. Bulgaria is saved from being landlocked by having the Black Sea on its eastern coast, which is also a generator of tourist dollars with its abundant beach resorts. The Black Sea is the country's lowest point at 0 m above sea level.

Bulgaria occupies 110, 993 sq. km (42,854 sq. miles); that is, it is slightly larger than Tennessee, Scotland or Portugal, and is home to 7,563,710 people (2009 figures, according to the National Statistical Institute). The country has seven major mountain ranges, (the highest point being Musala at 2,925 m (9,596 ft) and 12 national parks, home to historical ruins and rare flora and fauna. This means that there are great opportunities for trekking in summer for those who love burning calories outdoors (or simply picnicking for people who prefer a more sedentary lifestyle) and skiing in winter. Natural lakes can be found in the higher regions of Bulgaria and the country boasts over 500 mineral springs.

About 30 per cent of the land is arable, producing a variety of vegetables and fruits, tobacco, wine, wheat and barley and the much sought-after rose attar (rose oil) from the Valley of the Roses. Its natural resources include bauxite, copper, lead, zinc, coal and timber.

Bulgaria is one of the many countries that the River Danube meanders through. The Danube starts its journey in Germany, flows for 2,850 km (1,771 miles) through Central and Eastern Europe before serving as a border between Bulgaria and Romania and then ending in the Black Sea in Romania.

Average annual rainfall reaches almost 700 mm (27.5 inches), but in the higher regions, they average 1,000 mm (39 inches) and can reach 2,500 mm (98 inches).

THE WEATHER

Bulgaria has four distinct seasons typical of temperate countries, with hot, dry summers and cold, snowy winters.The northern part of the country has a more continental climate, while the southern parts and the coastal regions have a more Mediterranean influence. The physical relief of the country impacts on the climate and causes regional differences.

Average temperatures in summer is about 25°C (77°F) and in winter, it hovers around 0°C (32°F), although everyone familiar with temperate climate knows that it throws tantrums occasionally, so the mercury can shoot up or drop drastically away from the norm. Winter sports or *apres ski* enthusiasts will be pleased to know that snow cover in the

mountains can last for three to four months, from around
mid-December to April, although with global warming, this
might well decrease.

Spring

Although winter sports are still possible in spring if there
has been good snow cover, spring is also a pretty time of the
year down below in the lowlands with the mild temperatures,
the singing birds, the new-born ducklings in the ponds and
blossoming spring flowers.

Summer

Summer is typically hot, but made less unbearable by the
low humidity. Sofia, with the heavy traffic and endless
construction of roads and new buildings, tends to be dusty.
In August, it seems as if the Pied
Piper of Hamelin has been into
town and led everyone out to the
Black Sea or some other holiday
destination. Like their other
European cousins, the city folks
take their summer vacation with
religious fervour. For the radicals
who stay behind in Sofia, the
reward is that the traffic jams
miraculously disappear.

> Throughout the summer, it seems
> as if every one of the capital's
> inhabitants has either gone to
> the Black Sea, is talking about
> going to the Black Sea, or is
> hiding in their flats in the vain
> hope of tricking their friends
> into thinking they're spending
> the whole of August in some
> idyllic beach-side cottage.
> —*Sofia in Your Pocket*
> (a must-have free city guide)

Autumn

In Autumn, artists and wannabes would find the landscape
inspiring, as the leaves take on a golden hue. At the first sign
of rain and cooler temperatures in October, don´t mothball
your summer clothes. The sunny days can return and the
Indian summers in October are hot enough to require a
sun-block. But once the sun sets, it gets chilly quickly. The
temperatures in the sun can reach 22°C (72°F) , but may be
as cold as 0°C (32°F) in the mornings. So don´t put on your
woollen underwear, but wear several layers of clothing that
you can remove when it gets warm, especially in the early
afternoons. Dressing like an onion is the way to go.

The Miracle of the Sun

The sun in Bulgaria works miracles. In autumn and spring, what starts out as a chilly day with 0°C (32°F) at 8:00 am can be changed into a uplifting 22°C (72°F) by noon, if the sun decides to show itself. Similarly, a winter's day in the mountains in the sunshine can get as warm as 20°C (68°F). An outdoor thermometer is very useful to help you decide how warmly to dress, although dressing in layers is usually the most practical.

Winter

If you´re not from Siberia or the Nordic countries, the winter can be a real challenge. It can drop to -15°C (5°F). The first snow may fall as early as the beginning of November (which is officially still autumn). It can be a sunny 18°C (64°F) on 30 October, and 0°C (32°F) on 2 November. Winter in Sofia tends to mean weeks on end of grey fog, or with heavy snowfalls, making your way to work, school or the supermarkets a nightmare.

Although this park in Sofia looks pretty as a postcard with its light coating of snow, winter temperatures often drop drastically and make commuting a challenge for residents.

THE HISTORY

Located strategically at the crossroads of Europe and Asia, Bulgaria has found itelf the centre of attention of power-hungry neighbours throughout most of its history. Through sheer determination, much of Bulgarian identity and culture survived the occupations. However, its chequered history still plays a significant role on Bulgarian´s psyche and attitudes today.

Early Settlers

Archaeological explorations have found traces of human life in present-day Bulgarian lands dating back to Paleolithic times, or in common parlance, the Old Stone Age.

But a more settled population that made a mark in Bulgarian history came about in 6000 BC, where excavated Neolithic villages produced evidence of decorated pottery and clay figurines. By 4000 BC, the inhabitants were producing copper and gold objects. These original tribes of the Eastern Balkans were to later merge with migrants from Central Europe by the end of 2000 BC to become a collection of tribes known to historians as the Thracians.

The Thracians were a developed farming people, and were good at producing wine and breeding horses. They were also skilled horsemen and archers, with a fine collection of gold and silver. They occupied an area covering most of modern Bulgaria plus parts of northern Greece and western Turkey. However, their lack of unity was their undoing; their lands changed hands constantly, from the Greeks to the Persians, the Macedonians (under Philip II and his son Alexander the Great) and then the Romans.

Fans of Stanley Kubrick´s US$ 12 million epic film, *Spartacus*, with Kirk Douglas in the lead role, might be interested to know that the Thracian, Spartacus, is said to be from the town now known as Sandanski in southwest Bulgaria. Orpheus, the musical genius from Greek Mythology, was also a Thracian.

The Slavs and the Bulgars

The Slavs, an indigenous European race, came to present-day Bulgaria around the end of the fifth Century. Historians classify the Slavs into eastern Slavs (Belarusians and Ukrainians), western Slavs (Czechs, Slovaks and Poles) and southern Slavs (Bulgarians, Croats, Macedonians, Serbs and Slovenes). By virtue of their numbers, the Slavic language and culture soon became dominant in the region.

The Bulgars (said by some to be derived from an Old Turkic word meaning one of mixed nationality) are thought to have originated from Central Asia. These nomadic tribesmen had a formidable reputation as military horsemen. As early as the second century, some tribes came down to the European continent, settling in the plains between the Caspian and the Black seas.

The different tribes were led by Khans. In 584 AD, one of these Khans, Kubrat, understood that strength laid in unity and he managed to unite the Bulgar tribes under his rule. Byzantine chroniclers referred to his military and tribal alliance as Great Bulgaria, which is said to have covered an area from the Kuban in the east to the rivers Donets and Dnieper in the north and west and to the Sea of Azov and the Black Sea in the south.

When Khan Kubrat died, his five sons went their separate ways after dividing up the people, instead of staying united together, as their father had wished.

Khan Kubrat´s Lesson

According to legend, as Khan Kubrat was dying, he ordered his sons to fetch a bundle of sticks and told them to break it in two. When none of the sons managed to break the bundle, the Khan took the sticks and broke them one by one with his feeble hands. Kubrat´s message to his sons was that there was strength in unity.

It was the fifth son, Asparuh, who carried the torch. He led one of the Bulgar tribes west to the Danubian delta where he laid the foundations of the Bulgarian state. The Bulgars united with the Slavs to oppose Byzantine control. By 681 Khan Asparuh had forced Emperor Constantine V to recognise the first Bulgarian state, with its captial at Pliska, which was a combination of Bulgarian political structure with Slavic linguistic and cultural institutions. Under the successors of Asparuh, the Bulgarian kingdom continued to grow in size and strength.

One of these successors, Boris, converted to Christianity in 861 and Orthodox Christianity became the state religion. An independent Bulgarian Patriarchate was founded by Boris' son, Simeon, to prevent an over-extensive Byzantine influence through the church. The conversion of the Bulgarians to Christianity was facilitated by the development of the first Slavic alphabet, Glagolitic, in 855 AD by Cyril and Methodius, two Thessaloniki-based missionaries. Glagolitic was later simplified by their disciples to become the Cyrillic alphabet. The embrace of Christianity brought Bulgaria closer to Europe.

Subsequent Bulgarian kings were called Tsars after the Byzantine tradition. Under Tsar Simeon 1 (893–927), the Bulgarian kingdom reached its zenith, encompassing present-day Serbia, Macedonia, Romania and northern Greece. It was a golden age of artistic and commercial development. During this period, the capital moved from Pliska first to Preslav, then to Ohrid.

After reaching its peak under Tsar Simeon, the First Bulgarian Kingdom declined in the middle of the tenth century, due to Byzantine opposition and internal weakness. By 1014 Bulgaria was under Byzantine control. For nearly two centuries, Bulgaria was subjected to harsh Byzantine rule.

In 1185, two brothers from the nobility, Asen and Peter, led a successful revolt and established the second Bulgarian Kingdom, with its capital at Veliko Tarnovo. The brothers were later murdered by jealous competing nobility, and a younger brother, Kaloyan, took over the throne. Kaloyan successfully expanded the kingdom, before he was also murdered. A relative of his took the crown, but his incompetence caused substantial losses of his predecessors´ gains, before Ivan Asen II (1218–1241) got things under control again. Under his rule, Bulgarian territories stretched from the Black Sea to the Adriatic. Access to the sea greatly increased commerce, especially with the Italian Peninsula. Tarnovo became the centre of Bulgarian culture, which enjoyed a second golden age.

After the death of Ivan Asen II, Bulgaria was considerably weakened by marauding Mongols, internal feuding, and threats from Serbia and the Ottoman Turks.

Milestones in Bulgarian History

6000 B.C.	Neolithic settlements
2000 BC.	Thracians inhabit modern-day Bulgaria
46 AD	Thrace taken over by the Romans. Sofia named Serdica
end 5th century	Slavs migrate to Bulgaria
681	Arrival of Khan Asparuh; establishes first Bulgarian Kingdom.
855	Cyril and Methodius create Glagolitic, forerunner of Cyrillic
861 to 865	Khan Boris converts to Christianity, which was adopted as state religion
1014–1185	Bulgaria falls under Byzantine rule
1185	Peter and Asen establish Second Bulgarian Kingdom
1393	Bulgaria falls to the Ottoman Turks
1876	Revolutionaries launch unsuccessful April Uprising
1878	Russia liberates Bulgaria from Ottoman yoke
March 1878	Treaty of San Stefano (TSS)
July 1878	Treaty of Berlin overturns TSS.
1879	Alexander of Battenberg becomes Prince of Bulgaria. Sofia becomes capital
1885	Eastern Rumelia united with the Principality of Bulgaria
1886	Alexander Battenberg replaced by Ferdinand of Saxe Coburg Gotha
1908	Ferdinand declares independence and becomes Tsar Ferdinand
1912–1913	1st and 2nd Balkan Wars
1915	Bulgaria joins WWI, taking the side of the Germans
1941	Bulgaria enters WWII, siding with the Nazis
1943	Tsar Boris dies; 6-year-old Simeon ascends throne
1944-1946	Red Army invades Bulgaria. People's Republic of Bulgaria established.
1989	Fall of communism. Anti-communists create Union of Democratic Forces
June 1990	First multi-party elections
2001	Ex-king Simeon returns, forms political party which wins by a landslide
2004	Bulgaria joins NATO
1 Jan 2007	Bulgaria joins the European Union

Ottoman Rule

The Ottoman Empire expanded westwards and by 1393, Bulgaria had been swallowed up as well. The 500-year rule by the Ottoman Turks is the darkest chapter in the Bulgarian collective memory. The intellectuals and the nobility were the main targets; they were killed, captured or forced to convert to Islam, although some did so voluntarily in the hope of mercy or even a retention of status. The Bulgarian Orthodox Church came under the control of the Patriarchate of Constantinople, and all ecclesiastical matters were handled by the Greek clergy. A blood tax (*devshirme*) was imposed whereby young boys were torn from their families, converted to Islam, and sent to the elite Ottoman janissary (from the Turkish words *Yeni* and *Ceri*, meaning new and soldiers) corps. Only those who voluntarily converted to Islam (the Pomaks) were exempted from this blood tax. These difficult years still weigh heavily on the minds of present-day Bulgarians and they have not been able to exorcise these demons from their souls. One hears very often this phrase "We were 500 years under the Ottomans..." as an explanation for any less than desirable state of things.

> Let the Turks now carry away their abuses, in the only possible manner, namely, by carrying off themselves.
> —William Gladstone, on the Ottoman Turks' violent repression of the Bulgarian rebellion.

The oppressive rule was felt most strongly in towns. The centralised Ottoman authorities showed little interest in the villages, however, and they, especially the monasteries and churches there, became repositories of Bulgarian language and culture.

The National Revival and Revolts

The foundation stone for the Bulgarian National Revival is attributed to Father Paisii Hilendarski's *A Slav-Bulgarian History* in 1762 which documented the oral history of the people. Some historians (such as Ivan Ilchev) are uneasy at such a way of regarding history (through a simplified lens and seeing 'the past personified', in his words), but Father Paisii is definitely associated with any discussion about the Bulgarian National Revival. The book jolted the Bulgarians' national pride and in the next 100 years, they went on a path of rediscovery of their language and culture. At the same time, the strength of the Ottoman Empire was waning, and the Bulgarians seized the opportunity to return to the urban areas, taking up farming and commerce again.

Apart from a rediscovery of Bulgarian culture, armed struggles started to gain momentum in the 1860s. One of the most revered revolutionary was Vassil Levski. Between 1862 and 1868, he was a central figure in armed assaults against the Ottoman Empire. In 1873, he was hanged by the Ottoman Authorities in Sofia.

Revered Freedom Fighters Against Ottoman Rule
Vassil Levski (1837–1873)

Born in Karlovo as Vassil Ivanov Kunchev, he originally intended to be a priest. He became a monk 1858, but left the Church in 1861 to fulfil his revolutionary callings. In 1862, he enlisted in the Bulgarian legion in Serbia. He apparently earned his nickname, Levski (meaning like a lion) there for his bravery. Throughout the 1860s, he was active in revolutionary committees and armed assaults against the Ottomans. Caught by the Ottomans in 1872, Levski was hanged in Sofia in 1873. This Apostle of Freedom is revered by all Bulgarians (and often used by politicians of all stripes for their respective propaganda). Apart from his revolutionary zeal, Levski was also a prolific writer.

Hristo Botev (1847–1876)

Born on Christmas Day (hence his name Hristo) in Kalofer, Botev was a teacher by profession, but wrote extensively, especially revolutionary pieces. In 1874, he quit teaching to focus entirely on revolutionary work. Killed while fighting the Ottomans in 1876, Botev, together with Levski, remains a revered hero for Bulgarians even today.

In 1876, the Bulgarians revolted in the famous April Uprising, where tens of thousands of Bulgarians were massacred. Another famous revolutionary, poet and writer, Hristo Botev, led émigré young men and was killed in this uprising. Although the uprising was not directly successful, the Ottoman's reprisal massacre of countless innocent Bulgarians (including in the town of Batak, which was to become a byword for the massacre) galvanised reaction in Europe. American Protestant missionaries and British journalists were instrumental in shedding light on the atrocities, which led to politicians such as William Gladstone (former British prime minister) and public figures like Victor Hugo (French novelist and playwright) putting pressure on their governments to act. The American journalist Januarius McGahan's moving account of the horrors he saw at Batak after the massacre, the missionaries' reports, the urgings of the American consul in Constantinople, E. Schuyler, and the demands of many other British, French and Russian politicians and members of the public added on to the call for action.

The Liberation of Bulgaria

But there was no diplomatic solution to be found, and it was left to Russia to declare war on the Ottomans in April 1877. By 1878, they had liberated much of the Bulgarian lands.

The Treaty of San Stefano was signed on 3 March 1878, where Bulgaria was slotted to regain a large chunk of its former territory. Unfortunately, it was not to be, as a sizeable Bulgaria under the influence of Russia was worrisome for the other powers. On 13 July 1878, the United Kingdom, Austria-Hungary, France, Germany, Italy, Russia and the Ottoman Empire revised the Treaty of San Stefano with the Treaty of Berlin. Bulgaria was divided into two, with Eastern Rumelia remaining under Ottoman control. The treaty also required Bulgaria to choose a prince who was not from any one of the European ruling houses and who would acknowledge the Ottoman Sultan, so the job landed with Prince Alexander of Battenberg (a relative of the Mountbattens, which is essentially an English translation of Battenberg). He arrived in Bulgaria in the same year. In 1879, Sofia became the capital. Prince Alexander did not have an easy rule, with the interference of the Great Powers, especially Russia, and strong-minded liberal politicians at home.

Border of death

A recent documentary by German TV channel, NDR, brought to light a little known fact about Bulgaria's border. According to German political scientist Stefan Appelius, more East Germans died trying to cross the Bulgarian border into Greece during communism than anywhere else. The East Germans attempted the Bulgarian border after hearing rumours that the Bulgarian border was not tightly guarded.

Following agitation for unification with Bulgaria, an uprising in Eastern Rumelia ended successfully in a declaration for union in September 1885. However, this unificaion ruffled the feathers of both Serbia and Russia, the former fearing further expansion by a unified Bulgaria and the latter miffed that they were not consulted on such an important issue as unification. Serbia launched an attack but was defeated by the Bulgarians. Russia withdrew its support, and attempts were made to depose Prince Alexander by pro-Russian army officers. Liberal politician Stefan Stambolov countered the attempts and managed to keep the prince on the throne, but was later himself to become disappointed by the prince's pro-Russian posturings.

Prince Alexander had to abdicate in 1886, and was succeeded by the 26-year-old Prince Ferdinand 1 of Saxe-Coburg-Gotha. Twelve years later, taking advantage of strife in the Ottoman Empire, Prince Ferdinand declared Bulgaria's independence with himself as its Tsar.

Tsar Ferdinand led his country into two Balkan wars in 1912 and 1913, the first with Serbia and Greece against Turkey to retake Macedonia, and the second against its former allies as they could not agree on the division of the spoils of war. The second war ended with Bulgaria losing territory to Serbia, Greece, Romania. The insatiable desire to regain its lost territories induced Bulgaria to enter WW1 on the German side in 1915, but again, the country took a thumping. Ferdinand had to fall on his sword for the territory losses and reparations made after WW1. He abdicated in 1918 in favour of his son, who became Tsar Boris III.

Tsar Boris' rule was not any easier than his predecessors. The prime minister under his reign was Alexander Stamboliiski, from the Bulgarian Agrarian National Union, which favoured the peasant class. Stamboliiski also tried to forge a relationship with Yugoslavia, which involved renouncing Bulgarian claims to Macedonia, which was anathema to nationalists. There were also many Macedonian refugees loyal to the Internal Macedonian Revolutionary Organisation (IMRO) in Bulgaria at that time, who foamed at the mouth at Stamboliiski's making peace with Yugloslavia, which was contrary to their commitment to liberating Macedonia. These troubles, in addition to the fact that Bulgaria was punished by the Allies for its taking the side of the Central Powers in World War I by having to pay war reparations and losing chunks of land to Romania, Yugoslavia and Greece, meant that the political situation was a powder keg. In 1923, Stamboliiski was assassinated by right-wing military officers, and in 1925, an attempt was made to assassinate Tsar Boris as well in a bombing of the Sveta Nedelya Church that took many innocent lives. The political unrest in the 1930s was often met with heavy-handed response from the authorities.

As if all the internal politics were not enough, World War II loomed, and although Bulgaria tried at first to stay neutral, it capitulated and joined the Axis Powers in 1941 out of fear of a German invasion, as well as finding (again) the offer of Macedonia too tempting. One positive element in this unfortunate alignment was that even though they were an ally of Nazi Germany, Bulgaria managed to resist the pressure to send Bulgarian Jews to concentration camps.

Former Bulgarian king, Simeon Sakskoburggotski (holding flowers), was elected prime minister of the country and served from 2001 to 2005.

In 1943, Tsar Boris died suddenly and his six-year-old son, Simeon, acceded the throne, with regents ruling on his behalf. On 9 Sept 1944, the Fatherland Front (dominated by the Bulgarian Communist Party) seized power in a coup. Simeon remained on the throne for three years, until a staged referendum declared Bulgaria a republic in 1946. Simeon, his mother and sister had to flee to exile, settling first in Egypt and later in Madrid.

Communist Era

After abolishing monarchy, the Communists systematically crushed the opposition. Trouble-makers within the Party were also put down.

Georgi Dimitrov was the first communist dictator of Bulgaria, who did not hesitate to send political enemies and the bourgeoisie to labour camps. His Stalinist-leanings made Bulgaria the blue-eyed boy of the Soviet Union. A mausoleum was built in Alexander Battenberg Square in Sofia to house his embalmed body when he died, and was only demolished in 1990. After Dimitrov's death in 1949, Vulko Chervenkov took over. A faithful poodle of the Soviet Union, he was nicknamed Little Stalin.

The Rila monastery is regarded as one of the foremost masterpieces of Bulgarian National Revival architecture. It was declared a national historical monument in 1976 and became a UNESCO World Heritage Site in 1983.

The Aleksander Nevski cathedral is a historic Bulgarian Orthodox cathedral in Sofia, built in Neo-Byzantine style in the centre of the city.

Bulgarian cuisine offers a wide variety of salads, including the popular *shopska salata*. It is made with diced tomatoes, cucumbers and peppers, and topped with the famous Bulgarian sirene cheese.

Established in 1934, the National Art Gallery occupies most of Bulgaria's historic former royal palace, having moved to the palace after the abolition of the monarchy in 1946.

Houses built on the side of a steep cliff in Veliko Turnovo. Located on the Yantra River, the city is famous as the historical capital of the Second Bulgarian Empire and for its unique architecture.

When the tide turned against Stalinism, the Little Stalin in Bulgaria quickly lost power to Todor Zhivkov, who went on to rule Bulgaria for 35 years. A wily politician, he always managed to side-step political pitfalls. A number of repressive measures were undertaken during Zhivkov's rule, including the infamous 'Bulgarisation' of ethnic Turks in the 1980s (more details are to be found under the section 'the Turks' in chapter 3). His clever manoeuvres ensured he stayed in power until the fall of communist regimes throughout Eastern Europe in 1989, when fellow party officials forced him to resign.

After the Fall of Communism

His resignation was a cosmetic regime change and the Bulgarian Socialist Party (BSP), comprising many ex-communists, managed to continue a grip on power at the June 1990 elections, voted in by Bulgarians who favoured stability over free market reforms. The opposition and its supporters called for a purge of all communist regime politicians with violent protests. Another cosmetic change was attempted, by replacing the communist president with Zhelyu Zhelev, a Union of Democratic Forces candidate and a respected academic, but it was not good enough. The prime minister, Andrei Lukanov had to step down and an election was called again in 1991. The UDF won the elections this time, but victory was short-lived. Between 1990 and 1997, the government swung from UDF to Socialist and back to UDF again, as each government disappointed the electorate with a dysfunctional economy resulting in food shortages, electricity rationing and hyperinflation. It was only in 1997, with UDF back in power under the leadership of Ivan Kostov that some form of stability was experienced in the country.

Bulgaria started on an economic austerity programme of the International Monetary Fund and the lev was pegged to the Deutschmark in an attempt to control inflation. Privatisation of state companies started, although the sceptical population was suspicious that state assets were being sold off cheap to government cronies with negotiating officials being rewarded with attractive fees. The public suspected erstwhile and present government officials of lining their own pockets from the privatisation process while they starved, which was all too common in post-communist countries. Many former communist *apparatchiks*, meanwhile, were thought to be enriching themselves running successful mafia rings.

The disillusionment with politicians of all stripes, be they from UDF or BSP, meant that Bulgarians were looking for a figure of authority, untainted by the politics and corruption of the recent past. King Simeon II, the young king who had to flee to exile as a nine-year-old, then took the unusual step of returning to Bulgaria to head a new party, the National Movement of Simeon the Second (NMSS) and stood for the parliamentary elections of 2001. NMSS won with a landslide, and the world was astounded at the rare occurrence of having an ex-king become prime minister.

Although there were some murmurs then that perhaps Simeon Sakskoburggotski (the ex-king's commoner name) was using this as a stepping stone to return to the throne, the ex-king focused on improving his country and its image. His royal bearing and fluency in many European languages, and some might add gracious charm, certainly did no harm in Bulgaria's bid to gain entry to the European Union. In April 2004, Bulgaria became a member of NATO and in April 2005, Bulgaria signed the EU Accession Treaty, followed by EU membership in 2007.

Sadly for Simeon Sakskoburggotski, notwithstanding the positive gains Bulgaria had under his premiership, the Bulgarians were not happy. In typical fashion of the electorate in newly democratised ex-communist countries, they expected things to change overnight. Disappointed with the unfulfilled promise of the ex-king to improve the lives of the people within 800 days, puzzled by his quaint `exile' Bulgarian, and further influenced by a media that had lost interest in the ex-king, they voted for the BSP, which turned in the largest percentage of votes in the June 2005 parliamentary elections. The then 39-year-old Sergei Stanishev took over as prime minister. Fresh-faced Stanishev also appealed to the younger generation with his penchant for motor-bikes, cheeky humour and his ease with hi-tech communication. He apparently turned up at a party meeting in 2002 on a motor-bike in a jacket emblazoned with the words on his back 'If you are able to read this, Elena has fallen off on the way', Elena being his long-time journalist girlfriend who often rode pillion. Following his election as leader of the Socialist Party in 2001, he had an ICQ-chat with hundreds of users.

Two years on, Stanishev and the BSP remained popular, while the NMSS's star faded quickly.

In December 2006, a new political party, the Citizens for the European Development of Bulgaria (CEDB), was officially registered, and it became a force to be reckoned within a few short months.

The Royal Connections

The Bulgarian royal family is related to many of the other European royal houses and nobility. The mother of ex-King Simeon II came from the Italian House of Savoy, and his grandmother was a Bourbon-Parma (as is the current King of Spain, Juan Carlos). Simeon's grandfather, Ferdinand I, was a grand-nephew of Leopold I, first king of the Belgians. His great-grandfather, August of Saxe-Coburg-Kohary was a first cousin of both Queen Victoria and her husband, Prince Albert.

Simeon II himself married a Spanish aristocrat, Dona Margarita Gomez-Acebo y Cejuela. They have four sons and a daughter; all are married to Spaniards.

PRESENT-DAY POLITICS
First Elections for Members of European Parliament

The date 20 May 2007 was an historical day for Bulgaria; a day of many firsts. Bulgarians voted for members of the European Parliament for the first time. It was also the first time that voters could choose a specific individual instead of a party list, the first time that foreigners (if they were citizens of another EU country and permanent residents in Bulgaria) were allowed to vote, and the first electoral test for the new party, CEDB. There were a total of 218 candidates (37 per cent women) vying for 18 seats.

Although the elections were historically significant, Bulgarians were as lukewarm about MEP elections as their counterparts in other EU countries. The parties themselves treated the elections as a trial run for the autumn 2007 local elections, and almost all of their candidates for the MEP elections were unknown to the electorate.

Voter turnout was a lowly 29 per cent, although this is fairly typical of MEP elections in any EU country.

The Leading Political Parties in 2007

For political analysts, the MEP elections was a useful barometer to gauge the parties that had currency. It emerged that the top five parties were CEDB, the Bulgarian Socialist Party, the Movement for Rights and Freedoms, ATAKA coalition and the NMSS. Soon after the elections, claws were unsheathed, many heads rolled and unhappiness broke out in many of the parties.

Citizens for the European Development of Bulgaria (CEDB)

The popular mayor of Sofia, Boiko Borissov, formed this new party in 2006, which is known to the Bulgarians as GERB (the Bulgarian acronym for Citizens for European Development of Bulgaria). The party's manifesto revolves around the themes of civil liberties, Europeanisation, equal opportunities, family values and fighting crime and corruption. As Bulgarian laws prevented Borisov from being mayor and leader of a political party at the same time, the party's chairmanship was assumed by Tsvetan Tsvetanov, Borissov's former assistant when they were both at the Interior Ministry. No one doubts, however, that the party's popularity is based on the persona of Borissov. Born in 1959, and a former bodyguard of Simeon Sakskoburgg
gotski, he oozes muscled masculinity and has an uncanny ability to work the media and press the flesh, propelling him into the position of most popular politician (especially with the swooning women). Such is his appeal that an article in the

American Congressional Quarterly in early 2007 alleging he was connected to the Bulgarian mobsters only served to rally Bulgarians (including the president) behind him. CEDB won five MEP seats out of the total 18.

The Bulgarian Socialist Party (BSP)

This senior partner in the ruling coalition government has its roots in the previous communist party. In 1990, it was basically the old communist party with a change of name and which had purged a few hardliners. The economic meltdown of the late 90s resulted in a plunge in the BSP's popularity. Their fortunes improved under (current president) Purvanov's leadership and in spite of some loss of credibility in 2007 when the (BSP) Economy and Energy Minister Roumen Ovcharov was involved in a scandal (for allegedly threatening the head of the National Intelligence Service), the party remains popular with a large cross-section of Bulgarians. They managed a credible five seats in the MEP elections.

Movement for Rights and Freedoms (MRF)

A partner in the current ruling coalition, MRF has a strong ethnic Turkish supporter base. The party has been led by Ahmed Dogan since 1990. A skilful politician, he has promoted his party as a liberal one. The party has successfully played a 'kingmaker' role thus far, but things may well change with CEDB having leapt onto the political stage. Opponents tried to reduce the party's influence by successfully preventing Bulgarians living overseas from voting in the MEP elections, with a view to prevent ethnic Turkish Bulgarians living in Turkey from voting for the party. To their dismay, it didn't dent MRF's chances; the party managed to win four MEP seats, thanks to MRF's ability to mobilise its support base.

ATAKA Coalition

This is a coalition of far-right nationalist groups, which surprised many when it entered parliament in 2005. Led by tub-thumping Volen Siderov, a Bulgarian version of Jean-Marie Le Pen of France, the coalition won three MEP seats. Siderov's campaigns are basically rabid anti-Roma and anti-Turk rants.

Like Le Pen, his political support is not to be discounted, even if it's only due to protest votings.

National Movement of Simeon the Second (now known as National Movement for Stability and Progress)

The party's fortunes has ebbed considerably since its sensational win of 120 seats in the 2001 elections. Disappointed that life didn't improve by leaps and bounds under ex-king Simeon's premiership, voters punished the party in the 2005 elections, which saw it losing more than half its seats in parliament.

Others were disappointed by the party's joining the coalition led by the BSP after the 2005 elections, instead of going into opposition. The party's right-of-centre credentials were tarnished.

The party won only one seat in the MEP elections, an indication that the party has lost much of its lustre. The party changed its name in June 2007, shortly after the MEP elections, although the name-change had been in the pipeline for a while.

Other Parties, with Seats in Parliament
United Democatic Forces (UDF)

An alliance of anti-communist parties (including the Union of Democratic Forces), the alliance is basically an also-ran at the moment. After the poor results of the MEP elections (no UDF candidate managed to get a seat), the entire management announced end May they were quitting their posts.

Democrats for a Strong Bulgaria

A right-wing party founded in 2004 by Ivan Kostov, a former Union of Democratic Forces leader and prime minister, the party is also currently a spent force.

The Bulgarian People's Union

A centre-right grouping of the Bulgarian Agrarian People's Union, Internal Macedonian Revolutionary Organisation and Union of Free Democrats, the Union is another sunset coalition.

THE BULGARIANS

'Bulgaria has a special feeling for life—it's on the border between occident and orient. It is an exciting mixture. You cannot say, Bulgaria is a West European country. Serbia, Bulgaria and Romania are very strongly marked by the Turkish occupation. The culture, the music, the food-all of that is different. The way of thinking, too, like punctuality....'
—Ralf Petrov in *www.evropa.bulgaria, a book of photographic images by Doris and Juergen Sieckmeyer*

BULGARIA HAS FEATURED SO LITTLE in the international scene in the past decades, except perhaps as a satellite state of the Soviet Union, that a Bulgarian stereotype is practically non-existent. At most, perhaps people think of Bulgarians as a bunch of grim-looking communist types, living in squalid blocks of flats. While this may be true to a certain extent for some Bulgarians, they are a more intricate mosaic than being just ex-communists. The Bulgarian character is like the country´s geographical location: at the crossroads of Europe, the Mediterranean and Asia. Their Thracian/Slavic/Bulgar ancestry mixed with Turkish influence while under occupation resulted in a crucible of attitudes, traditions and superstitions drawn from these various sources.

There is also a difference between city and country folks, like in most countries. In the countryside, people are predictably more traditional whereas the cities are home to a more diverse group ranging from socialist die-hards to a modern crowd fed on pop-culture and capitalism.

The people´s dress sense runs the gamut from Soviet-era blandness to super trendy, some so chic that even Anna Wintour, the *Vogue* editor, would approve. The divide between the have and have-nots is stark; in the streets, manicured hands steer expensive cars past those left behind by the new market economy, some so poor that they are reduced to sifting through rubbish bins. Along the up-market shopping street in Sofia, Vitosha Boulevard, you can sometimes spot

There is an apparent rich-poor divide in the country; while the successful sport the latest fashions and expensive cars, there are still poor people scavenging to make ends meet.

some poor people collecting scrap metal and cardboard boxes in front of the expensive designer-wear boutiques.

The word `diversity´ is as apt for describing the people as it is for the country´s physical features.

SNAPSHOT OF THE AVERAGE GHEORGHI AND VELISLAVA
Physical Characteristics

If some generalisation is allowed, the average Bulgarian looks more like a Spaniard or Italian stereotype than a Scandinavian or German: they tend to be brunettes (if you exclude peroxide blondes) and are about 1.7 metres (5 feet 6 inches) tall without the aid of heels.

But when it comes to personalities, the reverse is true. They don´t have the quick smiles and open friendliness we associate with people from the Meditarranean countries, but are more reserved like the Germans, Belgians or Scandinavians.

The Bulgarian Soul

Because Bulgaria is a European country and you can't really tell if someone is a Bulgarian or Spaniard just by looking at him/her, people assume that Bulgarians think and react like any other Westerner. But Bulgarian characteristics are a little more complex than that.

Cross cultural experts like Professor Michael Minkov describes Bulgarian society as fundamentally collectivist, a characteristic more often associated with Asians. Group identity takes priority over individual identity. Family, relatives and close friends belong in the same group, and therefore deserve loyalty and special treatment. People outside the group are not only not accorded any special consideration, but are often ignored or even treated with suspicion. This group identification fosters a strong us versus them mentality. Such a collectivist characteristic can result in behaviour which Western liberals would term nepotism and cronyism. For collectivists, it is simply regarded as loyalty to your own community. This us versus them attitude also creates a tendency of stereotyping and even racism.

On the other hand, they would take in elderly parents and relatives into their homes if need be, without thoughts of invasion of privacy. Foreigners from individualist cultures

always find it remarkable that young Bulgarians still live with their parents, but apart from economic reasons, collectivists are not normally so concerned about private space.

Bulgarians are generally reserved with strangers. They are more like the fabled austere Germans (at least the image prior to the friendlier one discovered at the Football World Cup 2006), rather than a back-slapping, good humoured Californian or Sydneysider. But once a Bulgarian knows you well, he/she can be incredibly friendly and may pump your hands warmly or pat you on the cheeks when you meet. Those under 30 also tend to be more sociable and cheerful, as they have little or no experiences of the hardships endured by their parents and grandparents. City dwellers are also more introverted, but people in the villages can overwhelm you with their hospitality.

Many Bulgarians admit that they are a melancholic people, and who wouldn´t be, given their history? They tend to be dissatisfied with their jobs, health and life in general. In a Eurobarometer poll conducted in November and December 2006, Bulgarians are by far the most unhappy people in the European Union. The poll also found them to have the lowest expectations of the future. Sometimes it´s more than just melancholy, extending even to fatalism. If things are meant to happen, they will, and there´s nothing they can do about it, so they sometimes seem to be hardly risk-averse, such as the way they drive.

Society is hierarchical and patriarchal. Decisions tend to be made by those who are older, male, in more senior positions or in positions of authority. Like elsewhere in the Balkans, machismo is an attractive trait. Men may make cutting remarks about former female classmates looking like old cathedrals or old shoes, with not a single unkind remark about the males.

Patriotism, Nationalism and Self-image

Bulgarians have a strong sense of national pride. For most, it is basically that warm fuzzy feeling in their hearts when it comes to all things Bulgarian. Some are in-your-face patriotic— 'Sofia is the most beautiful city in the world!' or 'Bulgaria has the most beautiful girls in the world!'. At the extreme end are a bunch of nationalists, personified by Volen Siderov, leader of the ultra-nationalist movement ATAKA. A candidate in the presidential elections in 2006, he managed to attract some 24 per cent of Bulgarians with promises like 'giving Bulgaria back to Bulgarians through de-gypsization and de-Turkization'. Voters of ultra-nationalists are often those disenchanted with the current political and social situation, but it showed how attractive nationalistic spoutings was to a percentage of the population.

The thumping that Bulgarians have had in their history, and not being one of the countries that joined the European Union in 2004 have had an effect on their self-confidence, and one sometimes senses a certain defensiveness to comments by foreigners, even if no criticism was intended. Foreigners who mention how annoying the beggars and touts at Sunny Beach on the Black Sea Coast are may get a heated reaction from a Bulgarian, and

The difference between patriotism and nationalism is that the patriot is proud of its country for what it does, and the nationalist is proud of his country no matter what it does...
—Sydney J. Harris, American journalist

a demand as to which other tourist destination in the world has no beggars. Advertisements or travel guides of Bulgaria often adopt a cheer-leading tone, sometimes bordering on unctuous. 'Learn to say I love Bulgaria... Is it not true that love hides the shortcomings?'cooed one advertisement I saw on TV.

Yet, paradoxically, many are candid about the not-so-positive aspects of their country, and sometimes the level of self-criticism can be surprisingly blunt, possibly because of their melancholic tendencies.

Education

The literacy rate is high at 98.6 per cent, and as is typical of most ex-communist countries, there is no appalling gap between the men and women. The male literacy rate is 99.1 per cent and the female rate is 98.2 per cent. Many educated Bulgarians speak English, French or German as well. These factors make Bulgarians internationally mobile, prompting Bulgarian politicians to fret about a brain drain, and receiving countries fearing an influx of Bulgarians after EU accession.

Where They Live

Depending on their financial status, Bulgarians live in flats in buildings from the 1930s, one of the grim-looking Soviet-era

This grim-looking apartment block stands as a reminder of the country's socialist era.

blocks, or one of those spanking new apartment blocks that come with dishwashers and intercoms linked to round-the-clock security guards in uniforms. The wealthy have their villas, mostly with high walls surrounding them.

Most Bulgarians (estimated at between 80 per cent to 93 per cent) own their own homes, due to one positive feature during communist times—the ability to buy their own property. This explains why (apart from the Roma) there are fewer homeless people sleeping on park benches or in cardboard homes in Bulgaria, compared to many other cities in the world.

It's fairly common to find three generations living under one roof. Apart from the economic sense that it makes, it's also incredibly practical for parents who both work to be able to leave their children in the care of grandparents.

Bulgarian Names

Mr Tonchev, Mrs Toncheva and the Tonchevi family are related, even if at first glance, the names seem different. In

Bulgaria, the female members of a family add an 'a' at the end of the surname of the male members. When referring to the entire family, a suffix 'i' is added.

A less common suffix is the 'ski'. The female members of Mr Smirnenski's family have the surname 'Smirnenska', and the family is referred to as the Smirnenski family.

First names could be inspirations from Bulgaria's famous rulers (Asparuh, Kubrat and Tervel), typically Christian names (Nikola and Maria), or from Slavic origins (Vladimir and Velislava). It used to be obligatory to name children after their grandparents, but this is slowly giving way to simply the parents' fancy. It was also imperative that children take their father's names for middle names; hence, Ivan Sandev's son would have Ivanov as his middle name and his daughter's would be Ivanova.

And then there are nicknames. In earlier centuries, the community may give a nickname to a clan, a family or person based on occupation or characteristics. The most famous example is Vassil Levski, Bulgaria's favourite revolutionary son. He was born Vassil Ivanov Kunev, but given the nickname 'Levski' (meaning like a lion) for his bravery.

Those familiar with Eastern cultures will find it interesting that the Bulgarians also have specific terms for each relative based on how he or she is related to an individual. An uncle is sub-categorised into *chicho* (uncle on the father's side) and *vouicho* (an uncle on the mother's side).

Leilya is what an aunt on the mother's side is called. You might be surprised at the sheer number of sisters Mrs Toncheva has, when you hear her children calling so many ladies *leilya*. But, no, it isn´t that Mrs Toncheva had a very productive mother, but only that children will address their mother´s close female friends as *leilya* too.

Traditions and Superstitions
Bulgarians have a wealth of traditions which are still practised today, and even by the younger generation. That the traditions have been carefully handed down from generation to generation is not fluke but a conscientious effort to keep their identity in spite of (or indeed, because of) the numerous

invasions in their history. Bulgarian traditions managed to be kept alive in the mountain villages, as the Ottomans focused their attention in the towns. The result is that today, a cornucopia of festivals are still celebrated in the villages with the full splendour of traditional costumes, as their forebears did. In the cities, many traditions are also observed. But more on that later in Chapter 7.

Together with the traditions, superstitions also abound. The familiar ones like not walking under a ladder and not opening umbrellas indoors if you want to keep on the right side of Lady Luck are part of Bulgarian superstitions too. Salt wards off evil (you should sprinkle some on your window sill during full moon) and a black cat crossing your path brings bad luck (the antidote is to turn around three times in an anti-clockwise direction and throw a stone at the unfortunate four-legged creature).

Other Bulgarian superstitions are that flowers should be given in odd numbers as even numbers are meant only for the dead, putting a handbag on the floor would result in the owner losing all her money, dreams/nightmares only come true if you have them on a Wednesday, and placing a piece of the Christmas bread under the pillow on Christmas eve will help young ladies dream of their future husband; in this case, because it's Christmas, the 'dreams only come true on Wednesdays' principle does not apply.

The Fluid Bulgarians

If there´s one thing that irks foreigners most in Bulgaria, it is the Bulgarian fluid sense of timing. Bulgarians may show up half an hour to an hour later than the appointed time. Sometimes it´s not just fluid timing, but the reliability of what they say as well. Someone may call to make an appointment for lunch, promising to call you two days later to let you know the venue, but the day of the meeting may arrive without your having heard anything about where to meet.

The Women

As is typical for countries with a communist past, there are many skilled women in the workforce. Many Bulgarian

women balance working full-time with looking after the family. Some take on jobs which are considered 'men's jobs'; roughly 60 per cent of the tram drivers in Sofia are women. This entails their going to work in the early hours of the morning, and risking being the targets of criminals.

Officially, women are not discriminated against, but a glass ceiling prevents many women from reaching many top positions. Bulgarian society is still patriarchal, and the usual gender stereotyping persists. But inroads have been made in recent years, which saw, for example, Meglena Kouneva holding the position of European Integration Minister, and since the country's accession to the EU, becoming the European Commissioner for Consumer Protection. There are other women at the helm of ministries and corporations, too, holding top jobs such as Minister for Disaster Management, CEO of Bulgarian National Radio, CEO of Hewlett-Packard Bulgaria and Ambassador to the US. There is no doubt that there are many competent Bulgarian women and the mind-set is changing.

Women represent only about 3 per cent of the management of large enterprises and companies. In 2006, women in Parliament accounted for about 22 per cent. Women's salaries are also about 15 per cent lower than their male counterparts.

CNN presenter Ralitsa Vasileva represents the modern Bulgarian woman who has made inroads in the international arena.

There are still some darker corners, however. According to media reports, one in four Bulgarian women falls victim to domestic violence, and one in three has witnessed domestic violence or knows somebody who has been hurt by it. Thanks to the persistent efforts of women's NGOs, the Law on Protection Against Domestic Violence was passed in 2005.

The idea for such a law started after the Fourth World Conference on Women in Beijing in 1995. In 1996, the Minnesota Advocates for Human Rights (MAHR) undertook a human rights fact-finding report on domestic violence as a human rights abuse, and published its findings in Domestic Violence in Bulgaria (March, 1996). Further legal research by MAHR and the Bulgarian Gender Research Foundation (BGRF) followed on the issue and the gaps in the Bulgarian legislation. The hard work of MAHR, BGRF and a host of other Bulgarian NGOs was finally rewarded with the passing of the 2005 law.

Apart from the law, foundations such as Nadja Centre and Animus Association help victims of domestic violence.

There are other laws in Bulgaria protecting women such as the Law for Combating Trafficking in Persons and the respective changes in the Penal Code; and the Law on Protection against Discrimination.

Violence Against Women

"Until very recently, violence against women in Bulgaria was not perceived as a serious public problem deserving special legal regulation. Ignoring the extent and underestimating the importance of this phenomenon in Bulgaria has been due to a range of factors. The concept inherited from the previous regime that gender equality was already achieved in Bulgaria is certainly one of the reasons. It is combined with the hypocrisy of society, which accompanies such an inconvenient issue as violence against women. The deeply-rooted patriarchal stereotypes which characterize the Balkan and Mediterranean regions represent an additional factor. Furthermore, the persistent public/private divide confines women and the violence suffered by them to the private sphere of society...."

—Genoveva Tisheva, Managing Director,
Bulgarian Gender Research Foundation in *The Law on Protection against Domestic Violence in Bulgaria: Insights and History.*
http://www.stopvaw.org

The Youth

Like young people everywhere, most of the Bulgarian youth aspire to emigrate, assuming that the job opportunities that are lacking in their country can be found in abundance in the first world countries. Some 100,000 leave Bulgaria annually to study in universities in the US, Germany, France, Portugal and Malta.

Young people often seek education and employment opportunities overseas in the hope of better prospects.

For those who make it, the prospects can be very good. International companies are head-hunting those who have gained overseas experience to return to senior positions in Bulgaria, as they have the advantage of local knowledge.

The leisure interests of the youth are typically fashion, cars, skateboarding, pop music and discos or whatever the latest trend might be in the world.

The Bulgarian youth are by and large well-behaved, but Bulgaria does not escape the social problems present in other countries. There have been raised eyebrows in recent years at the increasingly flamboyant celebrations by high-school graduates (*abiturenti*). In May, you will hear a cacophony of horning and youngsters screaming as cars whiz by, with many young bodies hanging precariously out of them. Headlines such as 'Pupil Smashes the Head of a Girl in Class', 'Child Kills His Friend' and 'Daughter Slaughters Her Mother' are appearing more frequently in the local media. 'Happy slapping', the misnomer for the nasty practice of filming violent or sordid acts on a handphone, has also surfaced in the schools. Some of the acts involved the voluntary disrobing by teenage girls for the camera.

Health officials reported in 2009 that 67 per cent of the 4,000 HIV-positive people in Bulgaria were between 15 and 29 years old. Most contracted the virus through sexual contact.

Other reports indicate that substance abuse is on the rise, with one-third of schoolchildren between the ages of 14 and 17 having tried drugs (cannabis, cocaine, amphetamine or Ecstasy) at least once.

The Elderly

Bulgaria suffers from an ageing population. A report published by the World Resources Institute shows that the percentage of the population aged 65 years and above is about 22 per cent, while the share of the population under 15 years of age is 15 per cent. The birth rate in Bulgaria has never been high in recent history, very likely due to the inability to afford having a bigger family plus worries about the future, but

An elderly woman sells willow branches on Palm Sunday to supplement the pension received from the social security fund.

the birth rate has also been decreasing in recent years. As if that wasn't bad enough, the country has seen an increase in emigration by the younger people.

The elderly is probably the group that is the most disadvantaged with the transition from communism to capitalism. The pensions from the social security fund is their main (if not only) source of income. With the average monthly pension standing at 150 leva (approximatley EUR 70), they hardly have enough to get by, let alone lead a dignified retirement. Many depend on their children or relatives for financial assistance, rent out their flats, or resort to earning a few extra leva through selling herbs and collecting old bottles and cardboard boxes or worse, rummaging through the rubbish bins. EU accesssion will not change their plight, either, as the EU does not impose mandatory rules in this area and only recommends reform criteria.

The Mutri (the Mafia)

The average Bulgarian or expatriate is unlikely to be the target of the *Mutri*, unless you rub shoulders with the underworld, annoy them or are born under an exceptionally unlucky star. There have been reports of Bulgarians being shot dead

One unusual sign posted on the doors of Bulgarian banks is the 'No Guns Allowed' sign.

at close range in broad daylight, but they were all known to have links with the Mafia. A journalist investigating corruption also had his apartment bombed.

You can recognise the Mafia by the cars they drive (Audis or Mercedes 4WDs, often with blacked-out windows) and their physique (Arnold Schwarzenegger lookalikes minus the chummy grin), often sporting accessories like gold chains, expensive mobiles and peroxide blondes (these ladies are called *mutresi*).

The 'No Guns Allowed' signs on doors of banks are not jokes. Apart from the above-mentioned accessories, firearms are also a favourite accompaniment (only not visible).

The *mutri* are not afraid of anyone; not even the police. So it's best to stay out of their way, and never attempt to argue or fight for your rights if they jump your queue or almost run you over with their cars. It's their country, not yours.

Contract Killings

Bulgaria has been plagued by contract killings, which has done its reputation a lot of damage. In 2001, a record-breaking 21 people were assassinated. The victims are often allegedly linked to the mafia, although sometimes potential witnesses are liquidated. The authorities have had little success solving the crimes; in spite of most of the killings being done in broad daylight, there is an understandable lack of witnesses. Nothing much has changed since becoming an EU member; five months into its membership, three high-profile assassinations had taken place.

A Nation of Smokers

A Bulgarian who doesn´t smoke is as rare as a Yeti sighting. It seems almost as if Bulgarians have an eleventh finger—a stick of cigarette. In the parks, you will find young mothers surrounded by their offsprings, prams and a cloud of cigarette smoke, seemingly unconcerned about passive smoking.

Restaurants are now obliged to have non-smoking sections, but it usually means just the table in the most unsavoury part of the premises, surrounded by congenital smokers.

Bulgaria has a successful tobacco industry, so smoking is tantamount to a Bulgarian version of Harold Wilson's 1968 'I'm Backing Britain' campaign or both Tony Blair and David Cameron's 'Buy British' in 2007.

Status Symbols

The nouveaux riches display their wealth by owning top of the range Mercedes, Audis and BMWs, preferably replete with drivers. Canine displays of wealth are huskies, boxers and enormous St. Bernards which I'm sure consume more meat in a day than a poor pensioner in a month.

In August, no one who can afford a holiday should be found at home, instead of on holiday abroad, or at least at the Black Sea coast.

Spitting

Bulgarians spit for various reasons. When you see an adorable baby and exclaim to the proud grandparents what a beautiful child it is, the grandparents may make spitting sounds (without actually ejecting anything). Don't be alarmed; you haven't offended them; they spit to ward off any evil that might be attracted to their grandchild.

Out in the parks or along the streets, you may see people constantly spitting. If you look closer, it's probably that they are spitting out the shells of the sunflower seed. It's pretty amazing to see how the locals shell the seeds with alacrity. Around park benches, you can often see evidence that seed-chompers have been there. Others, like footballers, spit for spitting's sake.

THE ETHNIC GROUPS AND THEIR RELIGIONS

The population of about 8 million in Bulgaria is made up of about 83.9 per cent Bulgarians, 9.4 per cent Turks, 4.7 per cent Romas and another 2 per cent of others. Bulgarian officialdom prefers not to make ethnic distinctions, so the government website (http://www.government.bg) only has a breakdown into religious groups: East Orthodox Christians (85 per cent), Muslims (13 per cent) and Catholics (1 per cent).

Although the different ethnic groups don't engage in violent confrontations, Bulgarians identify themselves strongly along ethnic lines. Foreigners are not able to tell the ethnic background of a Bulgarian easily, except if there are obvious signposts like Islamic headscarves (although Islamic attire is rare in the cities) or the itinerant lifestyle or darker skin of most Romas.

The Bulgarians

This majority group are descendants of the Thracians, Bulgars and Slavs. They predominantly belong to the Bulgarian Orthodox Church.

The Bulgarian Orthodox Church

Christianity became the official religion of Bulgaria in 865, after the conversion of Prince Boris 1 to Orthodox Christianity. Boris' son, Simeon, fearing that the Orthodox Church might be used to further Byzantine interests in Bulgaria, established a separate Bulgarian Patriarchate. Its status as a national church meant that it wielded strong influence in the daily lives of the Bulgarians. This and the fact that the church and monasteries were repositories of Bulgarian traditions during the Ottoman rule, have resulted in Bulgarians identifying strongly with the church, not only as a religious institution, but also as a guardian of the Bulgarian culture. Hence, 45 years of communist rule did not make much of a dent in the people´s belief. With the fall of communism, religious festivals such as Christmas and Easter are intensively celebrated once again. Religion seemed to have only been dormant, not erased, during communist rule, and is enjoying a strong revival today.

The Bulgarian Orthodox church celebrates Christmas on 25 December like western churches, unlike many of the Eastern Orthodox churches which celebrate Christmas on 7 January. But apart from this, there is a lot more similarity with other Orthodox churches in terms of practices. For those who belong to or are familiar with western churches, Eastern Orthodox tradition is fascinating in its differences; there are no pews in churches, and marriage ceremonies are conducted around a ceremonial table with everyone standing. The ceremony is elaborate with the bridal couple wearing crowns, and music is not provided by a church organ (which doesn´t exist in Orthodox churches) but from the beautiful voices of the choir. Icons have a special place in the Bulgarian Orthodox church.

Hand-painted religious icons for sale at a streetside stall in Sofia.

Christians

There are small communities of Catholics and Protestants in Bulgaria as well.

Each church has its patron saint and believers honour the saints by displaying icons. Beautifully hand-painted icons are sold in shops in Bulgaria.

The supreme clerical, judicial and administrative power of the Bulgarian Orthodox Church is exercised by the Holy Synod, which includes the Patriarch and alll diocesan prelates. Patriarch Maxim was elected as Patriarch of Bulgaria and Metropolitan of Sofia by the Council of the Church and the People for the Election of a Patriarch which convened on 4 July 1971. His Holiness´ reign has not been free from troubles; in 2004, many of Bulgaria´s priests turned against him when it was alleged that he had close collaborations with the communist regime. Patriarch Maxim managed to prevent schisms within the church by taking control of the parishes in which these priests operated.

There are Bulgarian Orthodox churches outside of Bulgaria in Europe, the United States, Canada and Australia.

If you come across a Bulgarian whose surname is pre-fixed by the word 'hadzhi', don't assume that he is a Muslim who has gone on the pilgrimage to Mecca. It may also refer to a Bulgarian Orthdodox Christian who has indeed gone on a pilgrimage, but to Jerusalem. A trend which started in the 16th century, adapting the Muslim title *haji* to the Bulgarian Orthodox religion was done by the Bulgarian Orthodox pilgrims who wanted to have a title which gave them a respectable status in society.

The Bulgarian Orthodox Church

A wealth of information about the Bulgarian Orthodox Church can be found at their official website at http://bulch.tripod.com/boc

---

The Bulgarian Muslims

Some of the ethnic Bulgarians are Muslims. Called *Pomaks*, they converted to Islam during the Ottoman rule. Some say the conversion was forced, but others claim it was voluntary, in order to have the privileges accorded to Muslims during that period. The origin of the term *Pomak* is unclear; there are various schools of thought ranging from its being a derivative from the Bulgarian word for helper (for their assisting the Ottoman army) to harassed (in the opinion of those who saw their conversion as by force) to infidel (seen through the eyes of Bulgarian Christians). It is most widely accepted that it is derived from *pomagach* (meaning helper).

A large Muslim community live in the Rhodope mountains. Muslim women in the cities, especially the younger generation, generally don't wear veils or scarves. Those living in the villages may wear half-veils or colourful headscarves. Many Muslim Bulgarians are also not averse to drinking alcohol.

Ethnic Breakdown in Bulgaria
- Bulgarians: 83.9 per cent
- Turks: 9.4 per cent
- Romas: 4.7 per cent
- Others: 2 per cent

The Turks

In the 16th century, social changes in Anatolia led to large groups of Turks settling in Bulgaria and elsewhere in the Balkans. Today, ethnic Turks are concentrated around Shumen and Razgrad in the north, and in the eastern Rhodopes in the south of the country.

The 500 years under Ottoman rule is still seen by ethnic Bulgarians as the darkest period in their history and the present day ethnic Turks end up bearing the cross. The different groups generally don't rub along so smoothly. A lady I met at a dinner party said that her name meant black in Turkish. Mistaking the comment for Turkish pride, I asked if she was an ethnic-Turk, and was given a withering look before she replied that she and her husband were 'pure' Bulgarians.

From the birth of the Bulgarian state, the ethnic Turks have had their ups and downs. Many had fled during the War of Liberation in 1877, fearing reprisals once the country changed hands. To their credit, the Bulgarian government after liberation actually made efforts to preserve Muslim religious rights. Although there were cases of attacks by ethnic Bulgarians, there was no state persecution. Between the period 1949 and the late 1960s, emigration to Turkey was encouraged by the communist regime, but the Turks had a relatively harassment-free existence until the era under Todor Zhivkov. The early stages of his regime did not show signs of anti-Turk tendencies; in fact, Zhivkov tried to make the Turks join the communist Party. But the clinging on to religious traditions, was anathema to the communist regime. Additionally, their rising fertility rate and an increasing awareness of Turkish identity born of the Turkey-Greece dispute over Cyprus alarmed the regime. Starting with the Pomaks in 1971, the regime launched a campaign to `bulgarise´ all names, whereby new identification papers were issued, brooking no dissent. Resistance was put down forcefully. By 1984, it was the Turks´ turn. Not only were their names changed to Slavic-sounding ones, but mosques were closed down and the Turkish language forbidden in public places. It is estimated that between 500 to 1,500 dissenters were killed; others were sent to labour camps or forcibly re-settled. The term Turk was excluded from official discourse and replaced with 'Muslim Bulgarian citizens'. New history books were written to avoid the term Turks. This campaign was known by the euphemism *Vuzroditelskiyat Protses* (Regeneration Process). In 1965 a special team of scholars at the Bulgarian Academy of Sciences was set up to prove that all Bulgarian Turks had been forcibly converted to Islam and `Bulgarian blood runs in their veins´.

As Zhivkov´s regime tightened the screws on the Turks, many sought to emigrate rather than change their names. Turkey announced its willingness to take in Bulgarian Muslims and between May and August 1989, up to 300,000 Turks and *Pomaks* crossed the border. The flood of refugees became an unbearable strain on Turkey and the border was closed by the end of August. Back in Bulgaria, the emigration had resulted in depopulation and a loss of the people who used to harvest the important tobacco crop.

It was only with the fall of communism that Turkish identity was revived once again. Ethnic Turkish leaders at first joined the main opposition coalition, the Union of Democratic Forces, but personality clashes resulted in the formation of an independent political party, the Movement for Rights and Freedom (MRF), led by Ahmed Dogan, a university professor imprisoned by the Zhivkov regime for opposing the name-changing campaign. Although the party strenuously projects itself as a liberal party for all Bulgarians, its strong base of Turkish supporters has caused concerns that it is an exclusively Turkish party. The fact that post-communist era governments have often been made up of different parties cobbled together has led to the MRF being a `kingmaker´ party. Fears of the Turk´s perceived ambitions for greater power and perhaps even separatism caused nervousness in some Bulgarians and the extreme right, find the Turks a convenient target as they beat the nationalist drum.

Today, the Turks are free to speak their language and practise their religion. There are Turkish language newspapers, the official website of the Bulgarian National Radio publishes its pages in Turkish as well, and on Bulgarian National Television there are news in the Turkish language.

The Romas (The Gypsies)

It is hard to know the actual number of Roma in Bulgaria, not least because many avoid identifying themselves as Roma in view of the negative reaction it attracts. It is estimated that less than 5 per cent of the population is Roma.

The Romas are probably the most discriminated community in most European countries, and so it is the same in Bulgaria. Unlike the Turks, the Romas have not been able to organise themselves into a community with some political muscle, and find themselves living on the fringes of society.

Most live in Roma ghettoes, living a bleak life of little or no education, high unemployment and blamed for most crimes in the country. The 2006 figures indicate that only 10 per cent have secondary education and only 0.2 per cent have a university degree. A good 70 per cent of Roma children are educated in one of the 106 segregated ghetto schools in the country, which are sub-standard both in terms of quality of education and physical condition. With poor education, many Roma are unemployable, and they remain stuck in the ghettoes and the vicious circle continues with the next generation. Those who find employment are mainly in poorly paid jobs like garbage collection and road-sweeping. With the help of sponsorship programmes, there is an educated Roma elite of about 5,000 people. But stereo-typing and discrimination remain; educated Romas still face challenges when applying for jobs, or are prevented from entering a disco with the excuse that it's closed for a private party, and people instinctively tighten their grip on their bags as soon as a Roma is nearby. In some extreme cases, there have been attacks on Romas by far-right hooligans.

It has been primarily NGOs which have tried to improve the lot of the Romas. A self-help group, the Bulgarian Association for Initiative Business, which unites small and medium-sized Roma enterprises, aims to integrate Roma businesses into the Bulgarian and European mainstream. Government programmes to improve the Roma´s status have been sketchy and initiated only due to pressure from the European Union. Although there are two Roma deputy ministers in the current government, there are hardly any Romas in public service.

There are always two sides to a coin; employers say that experiences of hiring Romas had been negative, as they had poor work ethics. Some claim that Romas prefer to live off welfare than having to work for a minimum wage of 180 leva; others say that they are prone to crime.

The only sure thing is that the Romas are still far from being integrated into mainstream society.

The Jews

Although Jewish communities existed in Bulgaria from as long ago as the second century, according to some sources, the really large influx of Jews to the Balkans started after 1492, after being driven away from Spain. Many migrated to Israel after 1948, leaving a community of about 8,000 in Bulgaria today. An umbrella organisation called Shalom focuses on reviving Jewish traditions in Bulgaria and coordinates the activities of all Jewish organisations.

When it comes to heroes who saved Jews during the Holocaust, Bulgarians are proud of one little-known fact; that Bulgaria's 48,000 Jews were not sent to gas chambers, in spite of pressure from the Nazis. A book written by Israeli Michael Bar-Zohar, *Beyond Hitler's Grasp: The Heroic Rescue of Bulgaria's Jews*, published in 1998 by Adams Media Corp., recounts how Bulgarians defied Nazi orders and saved its entire Jewish population, even though it was an ally of Germany during World War II.

Bulgaria was, to start with, different from most of Europe, in that anti-Semitism did not seem to exist. The Jews were just one of many minorities who had lived in the country for centuries. Contrary to the Nazi's negative stereotypes of rich Jews, Bulgaria's Jews tended to be poor, non-religious commoners who blended into society. Things turned ugly when Tsar Boris III decided to side with Germany, in the hope of reclaiming Macedonia. A pro-Nazi government was installed, with the anti-Semitic Bogdan Filov as prime minister. Together with the even more anti-Semitic Alexander Belev, Commissar for Jewish affairs, the 'Law for the Protection of the Nation' was passed, which severely restricted property and civil rights of Jews and required them to wear Jewish stars. The Bulgarian Jews were on the verge of being

A synagogue in Bulgaria that serves the needs of the Jewish community.

deported when ordinary Bulgarians, led by some members of Parliament and the Orthodox Church, intervened. One of the members of parliament, Dimitar Peshev, in particular, is remembered for his storming into the Interior Ministry to demand the cancellation of the deportation order, and campaigned to save the Bulgarian Jews. In 2003, his heroism was recognised by the founding of an annual award named after him which is given in recognition of publications and broadcasts which explore topics on minority groups and ethnic pluralism in a positive light. The contest is jointly organised by the United Nations Development Programme, the foundation 'Multi-ethnical Initiative for Human Rights', Bulgarian News Agency and the Faculty for Journalism of the Sofia University.

The Armenians

According to the official census of 2001, there are 13,000 Armenians living in Bulgaria, while unofficial church data indicates 20,000. The exact number is in a way unimportant, because unlike the Turks and Romas, the Armenians are well accepted and integrated into Bulgarian society. Possibly, a common Christian faith helps, although the Armenians have their own Armenian Apostolic Orthodox Church. Perhaps it is the fact that both ethnic Bulgarians and Armenians feel bonded by their common history of having suffered under the Turks.

Bulgaria also played the 'saviour' role for the Armenians, by opening its doors to the flood of Armenian refugees from Turkey during the Armenian genocide between 1915–1917. (Note: Turkey has always disputed the use of the term genocide in this incident).

A Bulgarian whose surname ends with 'ian' is probably Armenian, and that's about the only overt distinguishing sign you'll find.

People of Other Colours

Bulgaria also has a small population of Asians (Chinese and Vietnamese), Africans (mainly Nigerians and Ethiopians) and Arabs (Syrians, Lebanese, Iraqis and Afghans).

Some have complained of discrimination, and in a few instances, violence. Dark-skinned players in the football teams have to endure being called monkeys, and local media reported an incident of a Nigerian forward of Bulgaria's Levski FC, Ekundayo Jaiyeoba, who was subjected to racist insults and repeatedly being called monkey, as he walked down Vitosha Boulevard, a posh shopping street in Sofia.

The discrimination faced by these foreigners can perhaps be explained by work done by a group of researchers from the Center for Migration and Refugee Studies of the New Bulgarian University, under the leadership of Assoc Prof Anna Krusteva: they are seen as 'yet-another-foreigner, who came to the country to eat the bread of the Bulgarians'. This may seem puzzling, considering how the Bulgarians have welcomed the Armenians with open arms. It might be that the Armenians don't look too different from them, and that they share a common Christian faith and problems with the Turks.

Stereotyping minorities is still considered a source of entertainment by the less responsible members of the media, so it comes as no surprise if prejudices colour the minds of the unenlightened section of the public.

Whatever the reasons, people of other colours should not be surprised if taxi drivers refused to take them or security guards in supermarkets follow and watch them solicitously, even if they're just looking at inexpensive items like cumin seeds and black pepper. A 'white' American, on the other hand, may be shocked by the friendly Bulgarian shopkeeper congratulating him or her for having the Ku Klux Klan in the US, as they 'clean up the country'.

If you're not 'white', it helps to be dressed nattily always and being a little more assertive than you normally are when among people of similar skin tones.

FITTING IN WITH THE BULGARIANS

CHAPTER 4

'We have a saying.
"You enter a country through the people..."'
—Sherif Ismail, Second Secretary at the
Egyptian Embassy in Sofia

As MENTIONED IN THE EARLIER CHAPTER, the average Bulgarian looks like a southern European. In sartorial terms, it´s also the usual Western style dressing, although colours are not inclined to be loud, usually keeping to safe neutrals.

Some foreigners (not coming from conservative societies themselves) have marvelled at the amount of flesh on display on some young ladies. The influence of Hollywood and fashion magazines have led to many young ladies trying to ape their idols, and it´s not surprising to see very abbreviated skirts and one-size-too-small tops in summer.

Many foreigners (primarily male) have declared that Bulgarian women are incredibly beautiful. Good news for male expatriates, but not welcome news for their womenfolk. Certainly if you come from a country where the women resemble Olympic discus throwers, the damsels here who weigh not more than 52 kg (115 lbs) with soulful eyes must surely cause the men to feel a surge of protective and other instincts. One male expatriate candidly admitted that it's all hormonal. But it is a fact that many of the young ladies here are a fashionable size zero, and very healthy-looking ones at that; not anorexic lollipop shapes.

Underneath the modernity and the similarities with other Western countries, the Bulgarians have a very keen sense of tradition, and it is exactly the survival of the traditions which makes Bulgaria so interesting, and not just another drab ex-communist country on its way to pulsating capitalism. The

Bulgarians are proud of their heritage and young people continue to dress in traditional costumes during festivals

people in the countryside are particularly observant, but many traditions are still practised by city dwellers as well. Christmas, New Year, weddings, funerals all have specific rituals that would bring good fortune, or bad luck if rules are not followed. Some beliefs are surprisingly similar to those in some Asian cultures.

Keeping the traditions was tantamount to keeping the Bulgarian identity during Ottoman occupation, and this is why even today, the younger generation in the countryside readily put on folk costumes during festivals to continue the practices handed down for generations.

THE FAMILY UNIT

Bulgarian society is family-oriented and the extended family forms a cohesive, dependable network of support. Grandparents help to look after the young when both parents work and a dutiful daughter will bring her aged father from the countryside to live in her small apartment in Sofia during winter, if he is unable to afford the heating. It is also patriarchal, so the eldest male person has a strong say in decision-making.

BASIC SOCIAL NORMS
'Yes' and 'No'
The first thing a foreigner must know to avoid mis-understandings is that Bulgarians nod their heads when saying 'No' and shake their heads when saying 'Yes'. Having said that, with tourism booming, many Bulgarians in the service sector are helpfully practising doing things our way even as we foreigners practise their way. The result is a lot of bobbing and wagging of heads that can cause total confusion.

Saying Yes and No
In Bulgaria, a shake of the head means yes and a nod means no. To avoid confusion, it's best to not only shake or nod your head, but also say *Da* for yes, or *Ne* for no.

Meeting and Greeting
Bulgarians are fairly formal, so American-style friendliness and use of first names are best avoided, unless they're your soon-to-be brothers or sisters-in-law. If you know the person's title (Professor or doctor) , use it, otherwise it's Mr (*Gospodin*) and Mrs (*Gospozha*), followed by the surname. If you think you will trip up on an unfamiliar Bulgarian surname, just murmur a greeting appropriate for the time of day as you exchange handshakes until you can get your tongue round Bulgarian. It's better than mangling up someone's name.

Gift Giving
When invited to someone's home, it's good manners to bring a gift, such as a bottle of spirits for the host and/or flowers for his wife. It would be a nice touch to bring some chocolates too, if they have young children. Note that Bulgarians are very proud of their wines (with good reason), so it's best not to bring a foreign wine. Whisky, rum or Bailey's Irish Cream would be a better choice. For flowers, they must be an odd number of stems, as even numbers are for funerals.

If your hosts are of modest means, giving an expensive gift will only embarrass them. Inexpensive but thoughtful gifts might include a nicely-wrapped hamper filled with home-baked biscuits, apple pie and/or muffins or items which are typical of your home country.

Gifts for a newborn should also be in odd numbers. You should not visit the newborn baby within the first 40 days after birth, a practice which stems from the old belief that a woman is 'dirty' in the first 40 days after delivery.

Gifts are usually opened upon receiving them.

FESTIVALS AND CUSTOMS

Bulgaria is full of celebrations and festivals, and most of them are connected to their pastoral life. The folkloric festivals tend to be concentrated in the rural parts of the country, but Christmas, New Year and Easter are celebrated by people in the cities in accordance with traditions as well. A closer look at the rituals for some festivals is to be found in Chapter 7.

Name Days

Bulgarians also place importance in celebrating Name Days. It's like celebrating a birthday with all the rest of the people who have the same first name as yours. This is a common practice in countries where the people adhere to the Eastern Orthodox faith. A Name Day is often a specific day in the year which is dedicated to a certain saint. Everyone named after that saint would celebrate on that day as they would their birthdays. Some name days have particular traditions associated with them e.g. on St. Nicholas' Day, a stuffed carp is served at dinner.

Opening Ceremonies

At ground-breaking ceremonies or the official opening of a highway, bank, shopping centre or school, priests are usually present to perform rites to bless the new structure.

Getting Married

Obviously different couples decide differently on how traditional their wedding should be, but on the whole, many charming traditions are still followed. Traditions may also vary depending on which region the bridal couple is from.

Traditionally, the prospective groom has to send an envoy (usually his best friend) to ask his (hopefully) future father-in-law for his approval. If he does approve, the father would have to ask his daughter thrice if she wished to marry the young man in question (I can hear the feminists cheering).

If all the requisite approvals are given, an engagement will take place, usually on a Sunday. Relatives are invited to a small feast, where details of the wedding are discussed. Stag parties and bridal showers are held prior to weddings.

On the wedding day itself, the groom picks up the *kumove* (the best couple who are usually man and wife, who are not only entrusted with bestman/matron-of-honour duties, but a godparent-like duty to help the new couple through married life). Together, they make their way to the bride's home. Entry is barred by the bride's family and friends, until suitably bribed with a token. All in good fun, of course.

On the way out, the bride may have to kick at a pot filled with water and some flowers for good luck, or throw a dish filled with wheat, coins and a raw egg over her head. If the dish smashes into many pieces it is considered good luck.

Then it's on to the civil ceremony, as no church wedding can take place before the civil ceremony. After signing the municipal register, the couple is toasted wth champagne, and pose with the group of family and friends for photos.

The church wedding comes next, and the bride and the groom should step into the church with their right foot first for good luck. As Bulgarian Orthodox churches have no pews, the congregation stands throughout the ceremony.

The bridal couple hold candles, as do many of those in attendance. The bride and groom also wear very old crowns and at a certain point of the ceremony, the best man has to cross the crowns back and forth three times, and the matron-of-honour has to do the same with the wedding rings, before they are placed on the fingers (note that Bulgarians wear wedding rings on their *right* hand). The couple then has to walk round the table three times, followed by drinking wine from a goblet and breaking bread. The priest conducts the ceremony not in a speaking tone, but in a special singing-speaking way, much like Gregorian chants.

The wedding ceremony itself is often rather short, compared to a Western Church wedding; not unwelcome news to those not used to standing for long periods of time.

Once the official wedding papers are signed, the bride and groom tries to step on each other´s toes, literally. It's not the first marital discord, but a typical tradition: whoever steps on the other's foot first will dominate in the new family.

Outside the church, guests throw wheat (or rice and birdseed) for prosperity.

The wedding reception is usually held in a restaurant. The newly-weds arrive last. If old traditions are followed, the groom's mother feeds the newlyweds a sweet honeyed cake and wine, symbolising a long and sweet life together. The groom's mother holds a loaf of freshly-baked bread over her head and the couple tug at one end of it each; the one who gets the bigger piece will have the larger role in the new family.

No Bulgarian wedding takes place without dancing. Usually a group of traditional Bulgarian dancers is engaged for the night, but everyone joins in the dancing.

Weddings and other celebrations never take place between 25 December and 6 January, as the Bulgarians believe that evil spirits roam the earth during this period. Bulgarians prefer not to go out at night during this period as well.

A wedding ceremony being conducted by the priest in the Bulgarian Orthodox Church.

Visiting a Bulgarian Home

When invited to someone's home, it's polite to bring a gift. Like the Japanese, Bulgarians do have a habit of removing their shoes before entering the house. Modern Bulgarians may not do so, but do be alert to this habit.

Compliment your hosts on their home, as Bulgarians are very house-proud. If they show you photos of their family, take an interest in them.

Don't recoil when Bulgarians ask you what seems like personal questions (your age, your salary, how long you've been married etc). It's an expression of interest in you and your family. There is no rule that you have to tell the exact truth, and you can deflect questions from yourself by asking them back the same questions or ask questions about Bulgarian wine, food and language.

The Dearly Departed

The family of a deceased will announce his/her passing by posting a necrolog not only in the papers, but on doors, lampposts and trees in the neighbourhood. It's usually an A4-size piece of paper with a photograph of the deceased, together with a brief message from the family, placed in plastic folder to protect it against wet weather.

It is a common practice to paste necrologs on trees in Bulgaria.

The coffin is kept open during the wake and funeral service in church. A close vigil is kept, as superstitions say that the dead person may return as a vampire if an animal jumps over the body, or a human shadow falls on the corpse. Usually 40 days after the death, the family go to church with a loaf of bread and some food for blessing and sharing in remembrance.

Ritual Bread

You might have noticed from the wedding and funeral rituals that bread plays a significant role.

There is hardly any important occasion that can do without making ritual bread. Ritual breads used to involve a specific process; they were made from the purest wheat grains and the flour had to be sieved three times, before 'silent water' was added. Flowers and herbs were soaked in the water before it is brought in by a maiden in absolute silence, hence its name. Tradition has it that the bread must be worked by a young girl or recently married young lady. Ritual breads have different decorations, depending on the event.

Nowadays, such a detailed ritual is no longer widespread but bread's role in important occasions is still significant.

The bread prepared for Christmas is known as *Bogova pita* (Lord's bread). It is decorated with varied representations such as pens full of sheep, wine casks, etc. depending on what the master of the house does for a living. Small rolls of bread are also given to the *koledari*, the young males in the villages going from house to house singing carols to wish the people good health and prosperity on Christmas Day.

Wedding breads are decorated with rosettes and doves, to symbolise good luck and blessings. The bride's mother kneads the dough for the ritual bread on the Thursday before the Sunday wedding. The rising dough represents the grounding of a new family.

Guests (especially in the countryside) are often welcomed by being offered a tray with a loaf of bread, from which they are supposed to break a piece off and pop it into their mouths.

HOW THEY VIEW FOREIGNERS

Bulgaria's history has been one of being occupied by foreign powers, or short-changed by them (think of how in 1878, the United Kingdom, Austria-Hungary, France, Germany, Italy, Russia and the Ottoman Empire superimposed the Treaty of San Stefano with the the Treaty of Berlin to deprive Bulgaria of the promised Macedonia), or bickering with neighbouring countries in the Balkan wars. With such memories, the present-day Bulgarians are not prone to being too trusting of foreigners.

In addition to that, the rush of British and Irish buying up property in Bulgaria has been received with mixed feelings; happy are those who have profited from the sale of property, but not so for the other locals who see these foreign property purchasers as taking over their neighbourhood and pushing up prices. Bulgarians who have had the misfortune of coming across some foreign drunken yobs are even more averse to foreigners.

Like in most countries, the younger generation are more open to foreigners, since they don't have such a heavy historical baggage. Pop culture also unites young people from everywhere.

Those of African and Asian descend are generally assumed to be poor and uneducated, or worse, illegal immigrants, so

may have occasion to feel very unwelcome. A landlord may refuse to rent out an apartment to a dark-skinned person, even if he is aware that the person is a diplomat.

Bulgarians and the EU

Bulgarians celebrated their joining the European family with fireworks, laser lights and a concert, Bulgaria Greets Europe, on 1 January 2007. The pride and happiness of becoming a European Union member state aside, many Bulgarians were aware that EU membership was no carte blanche.

Whether Bulgarians see their entry into the European Union as positive or negative depends on who you ask, of course. The politicians and businessmen may see it as a coming-of-age party and opportunities for growth for the country, but EU membership doesn´t mean much to people who are unable to reap the benefits of an open market. The pensioners are not going to see any rise in their meagre pensions, and the farmers don´t expect a sudden huge order for their products. If anything, they fear that prices will rocket, or that they will be strangled by the infamous EU regulations that sometimes even decide on the curvature of bananas.

A poll done by the National Centre for Research on Public Opinion between 6 and 12 December 2006 revealed that about a quarter of those polled were not worried by EU membership. This view was held predominantly by males, those younger than 30 years old, urban dwellers and wealthier Bulgarians. About 40 per cent of those polled were optimistic about the impact of EU membership, expecting that it would increase opportunities to work, live or study in EU states. The main fears expressed (mainly by women and those older than 50) were of price hikes in goods and services.

Certainly the elderly and the poor are hardest hit by EU accession. In compliance with the terms of EU entry, Bulgaria had to shut down two units of the Kozloduy nuclear power plant, which produced about 40 per cent of the country's electricity, due to safety concerns. The shutdown of the two units caused concerns about the supply of affordable electricity, and the income that was generated by being a regional energy exporter. Complying with EU regulations also meant extra costs for food producers, resulting also in prices going up.

For those who thought EU membership would be a passport to increased economic opportunities had their dreams rudely interrupted towards the end of 2006. Governments of many EU countries, mindful of how the worries of their own electorates might impact on their popularity, imposed labour restrictions on Bulgarians and Romanians. Only nine out of 25 EU countries offered unrestricted access to their labour markets. Bulgarian food exports face restrictions and Bulgarian air carriers are currently not classified as EU community carriers. Many of the citizens in the big eurozone countries also take a dim view of the two new kids on the EU block. In a *Financial Times*-Harris poll of 5,314 adults in Germany, the UK, France, Spain and Italy conducted between the 10 to 22 January 2007, only 25 per cent had a positive view of Bulgaria's and Romania's entry into the EU.

Whatever the views of Western Europeans, it wasn't about to stop Bulgarians legging over to these countries. It was reported in the local press that between January to April 2007, some 50,000 Bulgarians and Romanians arrived in the UK each month, quoting data from UK ports and airports.

Rila Monastery—a favourite with Bulgarians and foreigners, and with Bulgaria's recent membership to the EU, increasingly in the tourist spotlight.

The flip side of the coin is that with EU membership, Bulgaria is now a very attractive country for citizens of the richer EU nations to have affordable holidays, invest in property or retire, as the cost of living is still way below that of many of the EU countries. Bulgarian citizenship has also become very attractive for some. The *Sofia Echo* (English language weekly in Bulgaria) in January 2010 reported that 2,000 applications for citizenship were approved, double that of January 2009. The weekly also quoted the committee for Bulgarians abroad as having said that there is still a pile-up of 50,000 applications from the past.

The good news for foreigners in Bulgaria is that the days of a higher 'foreigner price' for hotels and tourist sites are gone.

For the Bulgarian who had looked at companies from the older EU countries as models of quality and reliability, their trust was shaken in recent years by some unexpected incidents. Austrian company Strabag won tenders to build the north stretch of the E79 highway and the new terminals and runways of Sofia Airport. Severe problems accompanied the projects, with the ceiling of the new terminal caving in and the tarmac on a runway wrinkling causing endless delays to the completion of the terminals.

Meanwhile, electricity distributing companies owned by Austrian EVN and German E.ON contributed to further ruptures of confidence when residents in Plovdiv, Varna, Shumen and nearby regions suffered blackouts and power surges so strong that they destroyed the residents´ household appliances in December 2006. Apologists have said that the low contract prices have been the reasons for the hiccups, but try telling that to the irate residents.

And then there is Natura 2000, whereby Bulgaria (as an EU member state) has to compile a list of sites to be included in the European Union-wide network of nature conservation sites to protect natural habitats and wild fauna and flora.Conservation flies in the face of construction booms, naturally, so there has been discord between green Bulgarians and developers who fear that their money-making projects will be hindered by conservation obligations.

The EU itself is still not completely satisfied with the country´s progress. The much awaited EU Progress Report of 27 June 2007 did not call for the imposition of the safeguard clause, but made known their dissatisfaction with the pace of judicial reforms, the fight against corruption and organised crime, and aviation safety and food safety.

Bulgaria and Romania

Bulgaria and Romania were obliged to work together towards accession to the EU, as their accession was a joint one. Although many were quite sure that both would make it into EU in 2007 for political reasons, neither country wanted to be seen as the under-achieving cousin.

Their joint bid led many people to think the two countries are like two peas in a pod, but this is way off the reality. They do share a Black Sea coast and the Danube, belong to the Orthodox church, and suffer from an image problem with Western Europe, but that's about where the similarities end. Foreigners generally refer to them as people from the Balkans, but the Bulgarians see themselves as Slavs, and the Romanians feel they're Latin. Like countries everywhere, the competition is keen among the closest neighbours.

I had the unusual luck of livng in the two countries in the last couple of years before they became EU members, and certainly saw a lot of differences between Bulgarians and Romanians in terms of what you might call mentality. The relationship between the two neighbours has not been warm and fuzzy, either, with the historic rivalry between them over the region known as southern Dobrudzha, which was occupied by Romanians between 1913 to 1940. In the first few months of our living in Bulgaria, we were still driving around in a car with a Romanian licence plate and used to joke that anything wrong we did would be brushed aside as 'It's only a stupid Romanian driver'. Some time later, we went into Romania with a car with a Bulgarian licence plate, and encountered so many difficulties with Romanian immigration officers, until one of them saw my husband's German passport. The officer started hollering "*Germania,*

Germania!" to his colleagues, and suddenly, we were waved through with smiles.

It's best to avoid conversations that seem to compare the two countries, to avoid trodding on sensitivities. However, with EU accession, a lot of Romanians have been crossing over the border to shop, stay in holiday resorts and buy up property (which are all cheaper than in Romania). The tourism and economic activities are leading to a better relationship between the two countries.

Bulgarians and the Macedonians

Macedonia has always been the bee in Bulgaria's bonnet. Bulgaria has gone to war over Macedonia several times, but without success. Bulgarians tend not to regard Macedonia as a separate nation, an attitude which the Macedonians see as pan-Bulgarian chauvinism. But all these seems set to change with Bulgaria's accession into the European Union. Bulgaria may finally be getting the Macedonian people (if not the land), as many Macedonians now want to become Bulgarians. The number of Macedonians applying for Bulgarian citizenship has shot up in the past years.

COMING TO TERMS WITH THE COMMUNIST PAST

As a former Soviet satellite state, Bulgarians today have to deal with the ghosts of the communist times, like many of its neighbours in the Baltics, Eastern Europe and the Balkans. Bulgaria has the dubious honour of being the last former Warsaw Pact country to open its files. In dealing with a country's communist past, one question that always crops up is whether to open, and if so to what extent, the old secret service files. The experiences of neighbouring countries showed how damaging the past can be for present-day politicians or community leaders. In 2006, Mona Musca resigned as culture minister of Romania, after being found out to having been an informant, and in 2007, Stanislaw Wielgus had to resign as Archbishop of Warsaw following disclosure that he had been a secret police informer. While some may oppose the opening of files to save their own

skin, others worry that doing so would destabilise the new democracies. Instead of working to bringing the country forward, politicians and the public could end up fixated with witch-hunts. The possible damage to the country´s reputation also caused shudders down many spines.

The question was hotly debated in the Bulgarian parliament, before it approved the rather curious provisions whereby the files of former agents would only be made public if their lives or national security would not be endangered, and only with the approval of the parliamentary commission´s chairman. This effectively meant that a lot of worms were still left in the woodwork.

But the lack of real public pressure to open all files suggested that ordinary Bulgarians had other things on their mind than dusty communist-era files, in spite of the controversy surrounding the apparent suicide of the head of the Archives in November 2006. When it surfaced that some candidates for the European parliament had connections to the erstwhile secret police, most of them did not have to withdraw their candidacy.

BULGARIANS AND RUSSIANS

The collapse of the Soviet regime has seen an influx of a different class of Russians into Central and Eastern Europe. In communist times, it was primarily the intellectual elite who worked in these countries. Nowadays, it's either the nouveau riche shopping for designer goods or the less-welcome types associated with organised crime or prostitution.

Ask an ordinary Czech, Hungarian or Pole, and it's unlikely that you will find warm and fuzzy feelings about the Russians.

The Bulgarian attitude is very different, however. For a variety of reasons, such as the Russians having been the ones who freed them from the Ottoman Turks, their common Slavonic heritage, a similar language, and the supply from Russia of cheap gas, Bulgarians do not harbour the kind of resentment of Russians as, say the Georgians or Ukrainians (in the Yuschenko camp). There are also no economic Russian immigrants in Bulgaria; on the contrary, many Russians invest in property or spend lavishly at the resorts. Such a winning combination has ensured a warm relationship between Bulgarians and Russians.

You might notice that some Bulgarians are latently anti-American; it probably has something to do with their devotion to the Russians.

OVERSEAS BULGARIANS AND RETURNEES

Many Europeans may worry about the sudden exodus of Bulgarians and Romanians to their countries after the two countries' accession to the EU, but in reality, as many as 800,000 to a million Bulgarians have left their country since 1990. The city of Chicago in the United States has the largest number of Bulgarians outside of Bulgaria. Significant Bulgarian communities are also found in Australia and Canada. In Europe, many are in the UK, Austria, Cyprus, the Czech Republic, Finland, France, Hungary, Italy and the Netherlands. Others are in Argentina and Uruguay.

Many foreign companies are trying to tempt these Bulgarians into returning to Bulgaria on expatriate terms to work in their Bulgarian arm. Hopes that Bulgarian returnees would change the worrying tide of brain drain is premature, however. Many of the returnees interviewed had not decided to return for good.

PROSTITUTION

There are plenty of shops around with names that don't need a rocket scientist to figure out what services they offer, such as Orgasm or Club Fetish. Many have secret rooms for such intimate services. Other signs are more in-your-face; they openly declare Sex Shop.

Services are advertised in newspapers and magazines, using not very subtle terms like erotic massage. They are usually accompanied by very graphic pictures, so no one really needs to work their grey cells to decipher the occupation of the ladies featured in the advertisements. Taxi drivers are apparently also very helpful in finding playmates, as are some hotel staff. One expatriate even claimed that his hotel receptionist prevented him from bringing a girl he met to his room and he swore that it was only because the hotel had their own supply chain. Prostitutes also hang out along promenades in resort areas and in seedy areas in the central railway station.

If you see a young woman frantically flagging you down on some main roads, it´s not necessarily a damsel in distress seeking your immediate rescue. Chances are she´s a prostitute hawking her ware. Bad luck for the real damsel in distress with a flat tyre on the highway, though.

ALTERNATIVE LIFESTYLES

Bulgarian homosexuals generally do not come out of the closet, except for a few pop stars and gay activists, as homosexuality is not quite accepted by society at large. Politicians and most ordinary Bulgarians give events connected to homosexual issues a wide berth. In October 2006, the annual conference of the International Lesbian and Gay Association (ILGA) took place in Sofia, hosted by Bulgaria's gay and lesbian NGO, BGO Gemini. At the official opening, the Dutch and Finnish ambassadors addressed

journalists and delegates. As a tradition, the mayor of the city where the conference is held addresses the delegates, but the mayor of Sofia, at the last minute, sent a short welcoming letter instead. A welcoming letter from the Justice Minister was also read out at the conference, referring to a new piece of law and a judicial system which guaranteed equal rights and protection, regardless of their sexual orientation and so forth, but refrained from attending in person. Media coverage was also lukewarm and brief.

Given the environment, there are no openly gay bars, but there are certain venues which cater to an open-minded crowd. Log on to http://www.gay.bg to find out up-to-date listings of parties and the like. Those looking for a support group can log on to http://www.bgogemini.org (BGO stands for Bulgarian Gay Organisation) for more details. Another useful site is http://www.sofia.gayguide.net to look for accomodation and other needs.

OPEN OR CONSERVATIVE SOCIETY?
In a patriarchal society, it is always better to err on the side of caution for women. Although the younger generation and people in the cities and at tourist resorts tend to be more open-minded, wearing too little material is apt to invite

Just like their peers in other countries, young women in Bulgaria may dress in mid-riff bearing tops during the hot summer months.

stares and unwanted attention, or worse, have people think you work in the oldest profession in the world. Women travelling alone in Bulgaria may encounter harassment, especially on international trains, no matter how modestly dressed. Yet, you will see many young ladies in abbreviated skirts and skimpy tops in summer, or young couples intertwined in very Houdini-like positions in the park.

In the Black Sea Resort beaches, naturism is also catching on quickly. Foreigners may be bemused too, by the number of old men and women who go to the public parks in summer and strip down to their swimwear, without any body of water in the vicinity (unless you count the murky ponds as a body of water).

The Pace of Life

Expatriates coming from hectic cities often comment that they enjoy the slower pace of life in Bulgaria. This view that the pace of life is slower seems to be confirmed by an experiment carried out by the British Council on 22 August 2006. Sofia ranked 24th among 32 international cities where the pace of life is concerned. Volunteers registered the time pedestrians took to walk 18 m (60 feet), as walking speed apparently reflects the pace of life. For comparison, Singapore, Copenhagen and Madrid had the fastest walkers, in that order. New York, London and Tokyo ranked 8th, 12th and 19th respectively. But if you´re in a hurry, the slow pace of people walking on the crowded sidewalks or the ladies at some supermarket check-out counters can be unnerving.

SETTLING IN

CHAPTER 5

'...Give us this day divine guidance in our selection
of houses, maids and drivers. We pray that the telephone
works, the roof does not leak, the power cuts are few
and the rats and cockroaches even fewer...'
—Anon, extract from *Expat Wife's Prayer*

Moving to a new country is always exciting and bewildering at the same time, especially for first-time expatriates. But even seasoned expatriates will go through some degree of disorientation, which results from being cut off from the cultural cues and behaviourial patterns you are familiar with.

Learning to speak a new language, finding out where to get basic things, how to do things, wondering if what you say or do is socially acceptable and so on is like trying to navigate a new neighbourhood without the help of a Global Positioning System.

Not a few European expatriates come to Bulgaria confident that they would not suffer from culture shock, as Bulgarians are Europeans, not baffling Asians or Arabs. But once they get down to the nuts and bolts of settling in, there are a few suprises. Apart from divine help, here´s a road map to help you along.

VISAS AND RESIDENCY PASSES

VISAS

These are the visa requirements for Bulgaria at time of press. For latest information, please check with the Bulgarian Embassy

- **Citizens of EU countries:** Visa-free for stay up to 90 days within any six-month period
- **Citizens of other countries:** Citizens from some countries such as Australia, Canada, New Zealand and the US : visa-free for stay of up to 90 days, within any six-month period

Types of Visas

- B Visa–transit visa (stay in Bulgaria for less than 24 hours)
- C Visa–short-stay visa (single or multiple entry) up to 90 days within a six-month period
- D Visa–for long-stay or permanent residency application

Note that:
- Payment may have to be made in Euros or US$, instead of the currency of the country you´re applying from
- Visas cannot be obtained at the border
- Your passport should be valid for at least another six months from your date of departure from home
- It may be a long process, so bring a book or a yoga mat

Anyone who has had experience with Bulgarian bureaucracy will know the difficulty of getting clear information. Even if you do get very clear instructions, the requirements are rather daunting. Below are the requirements at the time of writing, but they are ever-changing so I would urge you to please check again with the Bulgarian embassy and/or the authorities when you´re in the country. For citizens of some countries, the procedure is rather tedious, so do start at least three months before your planned departure to check on the requirements.

EU citizens

Membership certainly has its privileges. Since Jan 1 2007, citizens of European Union countries can enter Bulgaria with nothing more than an identity card. They are entitled to stay in Bulgaria for up to three months without the need for any other documents. However, there may be teething troubles so it´s still better to have your passport with you for the time being.

For a stay longer than three months, the EU citizen will have to apply for a `certificate for residence permit´, from the Migration Directorate of the Interior Ministry at 48, Maria Louisa Boulevard. The application must be made within three months after the EU citizen's arrival in Bulgaria. The documents needed are: ID card or passport, documents proving that the

EU citizen is working/self-employed, has a health insurance and sufficient financial means to support himself/herself, or is a student in Bulgaria. Family members who are not themselves EU citizens may also be issued with a residence certificate for a period of stay that coincides with the EU member´s.

Non-EU citizens

Citizens of some countries, such as Australia, Canada, New Zealand and the US do not need visas to enter Bulgaria if they do not stay for longer than 90 days within a six month period.

For those who need visas, there are Type B (transit) visas or Type C (short-stay) visas. There are different sub-categories of Type C visa, such as business visas and tourist visas and the required documents vary according to the type of visa you are applying for. These may include, apart from the obvious passport with at least a six-month validity from date of travel, proof of your medical insurance, an invitation from your business partner (in standard form available from the Bulgarian Chamber of Commerce and Industry), an invitation letter from your Bulgarian host (in standard form available from the local municipality), your return ticket and proof of your financial means.

Those who wish to stay for a longer period of time would need to apply for a Type D visa, which you must get *before* arriving in Bulgaria. You would need to go personally to the Bulgarian embassy to make the application. If you are already in the country, you would have to return home or make a trip to a neighbouring country to apply for a Type D visa. Applying for a Type D visa is a rather tedious process, requiring a mind-boggling amount of documents apart from your passport and the application form, such as proof of possession of financial means, proof of accommodation in Bulgaria, (if being employed by a company) a copy of the work permit from the Ministry of Labour and Social Policy, (if running a business) a certified copy of the company´s tax registration document, a certification from the court that the company is solvent and evidence that you´ve hired Bulgarians, (if an accompanying spouse) a translated, notarised and legalised copy of your marriage certificate.

Registration of Foreigners

Except for EU citizens, make sure you fill up a registration card at the immigration counter if you´re staying longer than 24 hours. Otherwise, you will have to register at the police station. If you´re staying in a hotel, this will be taken care of for you.

At the airport arrivals, you will have to fill up another form (thankfully a short one) at the immigration counter. The forms are sometimes issued to you on the plane; otherwise you will find them just before the passport control. Filling up this form saves you the hassle of having to register at the local police station, if you´re not staying in a hotel.

Residency Permit (lichna karta)

Once in the country, you have up to three months to apply for your *lichna karta*. This sounds like ample time, but in reality, it´s a rush to get all the requisite documents together, including finding your accommodation fast as you need to show your tenancy agreement. Most of the documents required are the same as those needed to apply for a Type D visa. For accompanying spouses who are not EU citizens, you will have to furnish proof that your husband is providing you with enough pocket money for your survival in Bulgaria.

The process is tedious which may involve having a document rejected, or request for yet another document, so be prepared for a number of trips to the Migration Directorate, which is staffed by officers who range from very helpful to those who seem bent on making life difficult for you. It's not that the Bulgarians have suddenly turned snobbish upon joining the EU. Before Jan 1 2007, EU citizens were subjected to the same rigmarole from the then candidate country.

Foreigners who want to avoid the hassles and can afford it usually leave the whole immigration process with a lawyer.

Tangoing with bureaucracy is part and parcel of the growing-up process while in Bulgaria. Foreigners learn to live with it, as the locals have.

ACCOMMODATION

When you first arrive, you will probably need to live in a hotel while you house-hunt. All the major cities have a good supply of hotels and as to be expected, Sofia has a wide choice. From five-star hotels to hostels, as well as apartment hotels with kitchenettes, there is something to suit every budget and desire. There is as yet no standardised system of allocating the number of stars to a hotel, and not all the rooms in an establishment may be of a consistent standard. Bulgaria is working on standardising the ratings and the EU will also soon start work on synchronised criteria for evaluation of hotels across the EU.

Looking for a Home

Sofia, Bulgaria´s capital, is the main government and business centre, so most expatriates are based in this city. Varna and Burgas on the Black Sea coast and Bansko, a winter sports resort, have seen an increase in foreigners investing in residential property. There has also been an increase of expatriates buying homes in quieter villages recently.

Modern apartment blocks in Bulgaria are well designed and provide 24-hour security; hence their popularity with expatriates.

There is no shortage of apartments and houses in areas popular with expatriates, as Bulgaria saw a property boom in view of its EU accession. In fact, Sofia and Bansko have been criticised for being overbuilt.

Prices are reasonable, by European city standards. A 180 sq.m apartment in Sofia city centre can be rented for 1240 Euros, and one in the suburbs such as Dragalevtsi would cost about 950 Euros to rent. Houses with gardens in the city centre are harder to find, but they are available in more suburban areas like Dragalevtsi and Simeonovo. Rental prices are about Euros 2,400 for a 400 sq.m (4,305 sq. ft) furnished house.

Popular Residential Areas in Sofia

City Centre
- Doctor´s garden
- Lozenets

Suburbs
- Bistritsa
- Boyana
- Simeonovo
- Dragalevtsi

Apartment or House?

Apart from the location, price and your taste, security should play an important factor in your choice. Unfortunately, foreigners´ homes are favourite targets, on the assumption that they are usually well off, compared to the average local. There are many reliable security firms, but an apartment on a higher floor is of course harder to break into than a house. Most of the new apartment buildings also come with 24-hour security.

Winters are usually bitterly cold, so heating a big house would be a costly affair, too. Depending on usage and the level of insulation, heating in winter cost around 700 leva per month for a 150 sq m apartment. Bulgarian property are not known to be strong on insulation, especially the older apartments. Heating was supplied by centralised municipal systems and funded almost entirely by the state, so no one bothered too much about insulation to reduce heating cost then.

As the weather outside is usually frightful in winter, having a garage will save you a lot of agony in winter scraping the ice off your car or trying to start the poor frozen thing.

Renting

Renting is relatively straightforward in the major cities. There are plenty of English-speaking property agents. When you have made a decision, the agent will give you a draft contract, which is in both Bulgarian and English.

Once the contractual terms are agreeable to both landlord and tenant, both parties will have to sign the contract before a notary public.

Much of the economy in Bulgaria is still grey, so don´t be surprised if the landlord/landlady asks for the rent to be paid in cash, or to the daughter´s or son´s bank account in another country.

Snap Shot of Property Sale Prices (2008)	
City	Euros per sq. m
Sofia	1000 to 2000
Plovdiv centre	650 to 2350
Plovdiv	480 to 1100
Varna centre	890 to 3100
Bourgas centre	950 to 2150
Bourgas	550 to 1500

Buying Property

In recent years, there has been a surge of property-buying by foreigners in Bulgaria, mainly by British and Irish citizens. Some buy property for their summer holidays, some for investment and others have practically brought all their worldly possessions to reside in Bulgaria for good. Sizeable UK communities can be found in the village of Avren (near Varna) and other areas near the Black Sea, as well as in the ski resorts. Increasingly, many are settling in small villages. The profile of these new British landed gentry ranges from young people clambering onto the property ladder, retirees looking to stretching their pension and parents who want a better quality of life for their children. In such `colonies´, you will not miss your Sunday roast, as some Brit or other would have started a pub or something similar to provide this British tradition for those pining for a taste of home.

Advertisements spill out from every conceivable magazine to lure property hunters. Some tell you why it´s a good idea to invest in Bulgaria, such as the low prices which are expected to rise after `acception in the European Union in 2007´, a `very high ration value/money´ and `political stability and low life costs´.

If you are bitten by the investment bug, do make due diligence checks before parting with your money. Property laws are national, so the laws may be totally different from the ones in your country. Consult the property professionals and lawyers. Some people have actually bought property off the internet; obviously there is a risk that reality is far less than what the picture on the internet seems.

Many new residential areas have sprung up, in Sofia, Bansko and the Black sea coast, offering a panoramic view of the sea/golf course/ mountains. While true to some extent, be aware that by the time you take ownership of your property, you might end up having only a panoramic view of the laundry of your neighbours drying on the balconies in the development next door which was built after you signed your contract. Urban planning is non-existent and the advertising slogan `coming next to a place near you....´ is true in this country, except that it should be taken with a pinch of scepticism; it may be a new shopping mall down the road or a building in front of your nose. Many areas are overbuilt, so there may be problems of the existing infrastructure being unable to support the rash of new constructions. There have been reports in some resorts of problems with water, electricity and/or sewage disposal. For investors, other issues to consider is whether the property will still have a good rental/resale value with so many developments around.

Mortage loans from local banks are theoretically available to foreigners; in practice, many banks are reluctant to lend to foreigners in view of the difficulty of verifying their credit-

worthiness and unfamiliarity of dealing with foreigners. Even if a bank is prepared to lend to a foreigner, the amount of paperwork can be off-putting. It appears that things are smoother for British citizens in view of the good job the British mortgage brokers are doing; other foreigners will have to wade through a sea of documents such as an application form, identification documents, a credit rating report, tax return, bank statement, bank reference, accountant's certificate, pay slips, employer reference, documents relating to the property and whatever else the bank requests. By the time the documents are ready, the property you are eyeing might already be sold off to someone else with the ready cash.

With foreigners buying property being all the rage in Bulgaria, many foreigners have been approached by total strangers—someone had a wizened old nun approach him—about available property in the neighbourhood. Some foreigners have been assured of a commission, if they helped to publicise the property.

Potential property investors can refer to a number of useful magazines and books on this topic (see Further Reading).

The Common Areas
One thing which you will quickly notice is the chaotic state of public spaces outside the home. As there is as yet no condominium laws in Bulgaria, people are not obliged to look after common areas such as the lift landing and stairwell.

Especially in the older apartment blocks, the common areas are usually rather dilapidated, but once you enter the apartments,

Note that mortgage loans are often no more than 75 per cent of the purchase price, although your entire property is encumbered.

there is a world of difference. A lot of love and attention may have gone into renovating the apartments, but no one will bother about what is beyond the front door. Old refrigerators and cupboards may be left standing on the staircase for ages, and no one can force the tenant to do anything about it. Thankfully, the newer apartment blocks are rather well-maintained and do not suffer from this problem.

Floor Numbering

Bulgarians follow the European system, so Americans should note that what you call first floor is known as the ground floor in Bulgaria. You will see in lifts a button marked with `П´, which means parter (ground floor) in Bulgarian.

Some Security Measures

- Don´t leave belongings openly in a parked car which might attract thieves
- It´s best to park your car in a paid parking area
- Install grills and security system in your homes
- Don´t flash expensive jewellery or your credit cards in public
- Be cautious of `over-friendly´ strangers met by chance in hotels, airports, train stations
- Ensure authenticity of company before you pay over the internet with credit cards
- Avoid altercations, especially with drivers of expensive BMWs, Mercedes, Audis

Utilities
Water

The cost of water is negligible at around a few levas per month for a four-member household. Someone will come by once every few months to read the water meter, which might be inconveniently situated in the bathroom, like mine. You will then sign on the book after the person has recorded the reading, and a bill will be sent to you later.

Sometimes, although infrequent, the water supply stops for about three hours or so, probably due to maintenance works. It's best to keep a few bottles of tap water on standby for washing in case a cut happens.

Gas

Gas prices have so far been very affordable, as Russia has been providing Bulgaria with natural gas at a reduced rate. But at the end of 2006, with Russia complaining that the deal was unrealistic at today's prices, Bulgaria's natural gas distributor, Bulgargaz, signed a new agreement with Russia's Gazprom. Under the terms, the price Bulgaria is to pay for gas from Russia will rise gradually until it reaches the average EU market price in 2012. So gas prices are expected to rise by about 10 per cent in 2007, and by about 40 per cent by 2013.

Electricity/Heating

Electricity was also provided at an affordable rate till end 2006, as Bulgaria produced enough electricity to even export it to neighbouring countries. But in order to comply with EU accession conditions, the Kozloduy nuclear plant had to be shut down, severely retarding Bulgaria's electricity supply. Electricity prices went up on 1 July 2007 to 0.157 leva per kilowatt hour (up from 0.146 leva).

In winter, heating/electricity prices will be significantly high. Heating in the older apartments are from a central heating system, so individual households are not able to switch off the heating. The heating runs from about November till end March, so on warmer days, you practically have to open the windows to let the heat out. It's a waste of energy, certainly, but this is a throw-back to socialist days when the regime provided everything and made all the decisions.

Most of the new buildings are not equipped with central heating, but each apartment has its stand-alone heating system which you can regulate. But the electricity cost for cold winters is rather astronomical. If possible, choose

EMERGENCY ⟶

an apartment/house which has very good double-glazed windows and insulation to help reduce heating cost (and noise from outside!).

Like water, sometimes the electricity supply is interrupted, although this doesn't happen very often. Torch lights and candles should be placed somewhere within easy reach should you suddenly have to grope in the dark for them.

Furnishings

There is as yet no IKEA. Many of the furniture shops either sell rather socialist-looking type of furniture, or elegant but rather expensive furniture.

Those who cannot do without the real IKEA will find the nearest ones in Thessaloniki, Greece and Bucharest, Romania. There is also a Romanian version of IKEA, called Mobexpert, which opened in late 2007 in Sofia.

WHAT TO BRING FROM HOME

Since 2006, shopping malls have mushroomed in Bulgaria, so there is not a huge problem about finding the basic household appliances, electronic goods, or things to satisfy the vanity in us (clothes, make-up, shoes). But note that as many of the appliances sold in Bulgaria are destined for the Eastern spean market, you might have difficulty finding an operation manual in English or another West European language. They are usually in Bulgarian, Czech, Hungarian, Romanian and other exotic eastern European languages. So when you buy electronic goods in Bulgaria, ask first if there are instructions in English.

Some expatriates like to bring their own things with them, in order to re-create the feel of home in a new country. Others prefer to rent a furnished apartment to avoid the hassles of worrying about shipping things from one country to another, with the possible risk of things getting lost in transit.

If you decide to bring your household appliances, note that Bulgaria's electricity supply is 220 volts, and the continental two-pin plugs are used. So Americans and Canadians will need to arm themselves with a transformer and Australians, Britons, Irish, New Zealanders, South Africans and all who use the three-pin plug will need adaptors.

Apart from the main equipment, you should bring stock of the parts that need constant replacements e.g. the disposable vacuum bags of a vacuum cleaner. You might not so readily find the right shape and size to fit your vacuum cleaner.

Voltage, Plugs and Accessories
If you're bringing your own electronic goods:
- It's 220 v, and two-pin plugs here, so bring transformers and adaptors as required
- Bring a stock of vacuum bags. Bags are available in 'technomarkets', but it may take time to find the one that fits your vacuum cleaner perfectly

---

What you do need to bring from home are important documents like marriage certificates, insurance documents and documents relating to the children's education (if they will be going to school in Bulgaria). They may not be needed, but with the bureaucrats, it's always better to be prepared. Documents that are very likely to be needed to apply for residency permits (e.g. marriage certificates and children´s birth certificates, if you and your spouse have different nationalities) should be translated into Bulgarian, notarised and legalised. Note that as child-trafficking is a serious problem in the region, you are sometimes required to prove that you are the legal parent at immigration checkpoints, especially if you have a different nationality from your children.

While English language novels, newspapers and magazines are available, those pertaining to a special industry or area of interest are limited.

If you wear glasses or contact lenses, it also makes sense to bring an extra pair of glasses/ stock of disposable lenses. While there are competent opticians and opthalmologists here, the last thing you need is to have to spend time getting new glasses or lenses in a country you are as yet unfamiliar with.

Germans and Belgians who can´t imagine a garden without garden gnomes need not lug theirs along; Bulgarians share a similar interest and there are enough garden gnomes for sale here.

MEDIA

Bulgarian language newspapers are a dime a dozen. Foreigners who are unable to read Bulgarian but would like to know what´s going on in their host country can turn to the *Sofia Echo* (a weekly newspaper in English) and the *Bulgarisches Wirtschaftsblatt und Südosteuropäischer Report* (a monthly German-language newspaper). There are also various magazines and online media with good coverage of the important news which you can turn to (listed in Resource Guide).

Foreign newspapers and magazines are available at newstands in major hotels and shopping centres such as TZUM and City Centre Sofia. Two newsstands at the end of Vitosha Boulevard (in the vicinity of the Sveta Nedelya Church) also have a selection of foreign language reading material). There is a wider range of English and German newspapers and magazines than in any other foreign languages, reflecting the fact that the two biggest foreign communities here are the English and the German-speaking ones. The staples of *Time, Newsweek, Economist, International Herald Tribune* and

A rare antique newsstand in the city centre of Sofia.

Financial Times are available, as are entertainment magazines like *People* and *Hello!*.

Delivery of subscriptions may not arrive like clockwork. Sometimes your newspaper that comes out on a Friday may reach you on Wednesday, and there were occasions when my *Economist* for the week didn´t show up, but came together with the next week´s issue. There´s a German saying that there´s nothing older than yesterday´s newspapers; if you´re a believer of the saying, it´s irritating. When there is a public holiday, you can expect your subscriptions to arrive late. The irony is that the paper/magazine is available on the newstands, but not delivered to the subscriber on time.

SCHOOLS

Bulgaria has basically three types of schools: state, municipal and private. There are quite a few which have a strong focus on foreign languages such as English and German. Russian was compulsory up till 1989, but few opt for this language in school nowadays.

If you´re living in Sofia, there are quite a few international schools which are popular with expatriates, such as the Anglo-American School, The American English Academy, Le Lycée Victor Hugo (French) and Deutsche Schule Erich Kästner

(German). Expatriate friends tell me that Victor Hugo and Erich Kästner have a substantial number of Bulgarian children, so non-Bulgarian students may find that once outside of the classroom, friendships and communication with Bulgarian classmates may be hampered by the Bulgarians´ preference for lapsing into their own tongue.

Outside of Sofia, you will have to depend on the local schools. For expatriate children, local schools will be tricky as Bulgarian language proficiency is required.

The campus of Sofia University, one of several in Bulgaria that offer tertiary-level education.

DOMESTIC HELP

Affordable domestic help is readily available in Bulgaria. Salary scales in Bulgaria are very modest, so you may find educated people working as domestic helpers. Finding reliable and trustworthy domestic help is always the harder part; expatriates usually use the person cleaning the office (or a recommendation from that person), take over the domestic helper of a predecessor, or ask colleagues and friends for recommendations. The International Women´s Club in Sofia is another source to check with.

There is a lifestyle management, concierge service and property management (in their own words) company that provides services ranging from daily cleaning, running errands to lift maintenance and event planning. Their website is: http://www.todoor.net. Another company offering services ranging from domestic services to taxation consultancy can be contacted at tel: 08888 07911.

MODES OF TRANSPORT
Driving

Bulgarians drive on the right-hand side of the road, and drivers sit on the left-hand side of the car. So those coming from countries such as UK, Australia, New Zealand, South Africa, India and Pakistan will have to get used to driving on the `wrong´ side of the road. Foreigners will also have to get used to the signs which are only in Cyrillic, except on the highways where the names are in Roman letters too.

Most roads in Bulgaria unfortunately leaves much to be desired. Potholes, narrow streets, lack of planning makes driving a challenge, although things are improving with EU funds. If the road conditions are not enough to give you a few grey hairs, the Bulgarian drivers will see to it that you have an exciting experience. Bulgarian drivers seem to think they are on a Formula One racing track as soon as they get behind the wheels, never mind the above-mentioned obstacles and the (in)capacity of their cars.

Except for the month of August, when everyone seems to have gone on holiday, Sofia city centre is simply stand-still traffic on weekdays. All drivers in Sofia (who have never been

to Bangkok, Cairo or Naples) complain about the horrible jams. Bulgarians feel it is an achievement to get just one car length ahead, so drivers behind you will squeeze their way past you, and they'll do it even if it means driving on the lane with oncoming traffic. I once saw a man driving on the tracks meant for the tram, in the wrong direction and with a child standing in the back between the two front seats. A crash would have catapulted the child straight through the windscreen.

At traffic lights, cars will nonchalantly edge their way past the first car in the queue and actually wait in the area beyond the lights. When the lights turn green, they are not able to see that, so the cars behind will set off a cacophony of tooting of horns. If you find yourself caught in a wrong lane, which is highly probable when you first arrive, there will be much angry gesticulations in your direction. Having a diplomatic plate (obvious as it is red in colour, as opposed to the white plates of ordinary folks) is no guarantee of restraint from agitated Bulgarians, one who showed us his middle finger. But don´t get mad when you hear a constant horning sometimes, especially on Saturdays, as it could be only a happy bridal entourage passing by.

Driving in the city is a hair-raising experience, but the country roads will work up even more of your adrenalin. The harsh extremes of temperature really rough up the roads, and

Those who choose to drive in Bulgaria will have to contend with the congested roads which are poorly planned and not well maintained.

since repairs have been lacking due to insufficient funds, the roads are reminiscent of moonscape. As most of the roads have only one lane, and narrow to boot, cars have to crawl carefully over the craters, or swerve suddenly to avoid landing in them. The road conditions in no way slow down the manic drivers, however. When stuck behind an over-loaded, slow-moving truck, they will perform any manoeuvre just to overtake. Sometimes, you will find horse-driven carts or animals moseying along on the roads. Given these conditions, it´s advisable to avoid driving in the night, if possible. Road signs may also go missing; stolen to be sold as scrap iron at the rate of about 10 to 30 stotinki per kg.

Cars may flash their headlights at you for different reasons. If it´s a big, expensive car you see in your rear-view mirror flashing its lights, it means `get out of my way NOW!´ If cars coming in the opposite direction make a few quick flashes of light, it means `Look out, radar speed traps/police ahead!´ After all these harrowing country roads and crowded, narrow roads in the centre of Sofia, the highways are a welcome change. As at 2007, only two per cent of Bulgaria roads are highways and 16 per cent are considered `first class´. The highways are in good condition, courtesy of EU funds, and are well sign-posted in both Bulgarian and English. There is a petrol station every 10 to 20 km, many of which have modern snack shops within.

Watch out, though, for cars suddenly jamming on their brakes. As soon as a Bulgarian sees or is warned by fellow drivers that there are traffic cops ahead, he/she will slow down drastically.

Many of the major roads outside the city require `vignettes´. Different types of vignettes are available: annual (67 leva), monthly (25 leva) or weekly (10 leva). These can be bought from post offices and most petrol stations. Drivers have complained that annual vignettes are practically unavailable, and that the petrol stations sell only the monthly or weekly vignettes which works out to be more expensive in the end. Drivers suspect the petrol stations hide the annual vignettes to force drivers to buy the more expensive vignettes (as they get a percentage from the vignette price).

The type of cars available in Bulgaria range from Maserati (there´s a posh showroom next to City Centre Sofia), Mercedes, Audi and BMW to the humble Trabant produced in the former East Germany.

Buying and renting cars are relatively uncomplicated if you go to a reputable dealer or rental companies. Car rental companies like Avis, Thrifty, Sixt and Europcar have offices in most major cities or are represented by travel agents. Car rental desks can also be found in the lobbies of larger hotels. There are also local car rental companies, but their fleet of cars may not be as well maintained as those of the international companies.

Driving into Bulgaria

If your drive into Bulgaria from another country (including EU countries), make sure you bring the original registration and ownership documents apart from having a valid driving licence and insurance cover. Note that your car and your passport details are duly recorded, so you can´t leave the country without your car. This is apparently done to stem the car thefts in the country, although I´ve never heard of anyone managing to recover a stolen car so far. If you intend to leave the country without your car, there are customs procedures to follow, including leaving your car with them.

If you drive into Bulgaria, and someone else is driving the car out of the country without you, make sure the car is ´registered´ with him/her as well. My husband drove into Bulgaria from Romania in a Romanian registered car and this was duly recorded by border officials. When his Romanian colleague took the car back to Romania alone, he was stopped at the border. The car was left at the border and he walked across the checkpoint to be picked up by his father. My husband then had to go to the border the next day just to drive the car across the border and walk back to Bulgaria across the checkpoint.

There have been cases of highway robbery, and cars with foreign licence plates are favourite targets. If you must drive into Bulgaria, do it during daylight hours and preferably in a group.

Driving in Winter Conditions

From 1 November to 1 March, Bulgarian laws require headlights to be switched on all day, even if the sun is shining.

Take all the necessary winter precautions when driving in winter. It is advisable to change into winter tyres in early November. If you wait till the first snow falls, there will be long queues at the workshops. If you´re driving up to the mountains, make sure you have snow chains. A 50-50 mix of antifreeze and water in the cooling system is recommended in winter. Windscreen washer fluid should be topped up and treated with a proprietary additive (not engine anti-freeze) to reduce the possibility of freezing. Have warm rugs in the car in case your car stalls and you have to wait for help in the cold, which may take some time. An old rug in the car will come in handy to slip under the tyres if the car does get stuck.

Stopping distances in snow and ice are ten times longer than on normal road conditions.

Although always essential to have with you, it´s even more important in winter to make sure you have the staples of a fully loaded handphone, torch light and batteries, first aid kit, warning triangle, traffic safety vests, tow ropes, jump leads, water and food.

Driving Licence

Foreigners can drive in Bulgaria using their national driving licence for up to one year. It´s always better to err on the side of caution and have an international driving licence as well, which you can get from your local AA office.

In 2007, tests to get a driving licence conducted in English became available. The trail-blazing first five foreigners (all Indian nationals working in a steel plant) to sit for the test all failed. Driving licences for foreigners are only available for long-term residents.

Parking and Car Theft

With the congestion, finding a parking lot in the city centre of Sofia is like winning the lottery. There are a number of paid parking areas, but most cars are left on the pavements, risking being clamped or towed away.

A substantial part of Sofia city centre is a `blue parking zone´; you need to buy vouchers from the parking attendants or nearby shops, validate them and display them on your car window. Since mid 2007, you can alternatively pay by sending an SMS, if you have an account with a local GSM operator. The instructions on the vouchers are only in Bulgarian. Failure to display such a voucher risks having your car towed away or clamped.

Car theft is a real problem in Bulgaria, so it makes sense to park in a paid car-park or at least avoid a quiet, obscure side street. Opting for a more modest car may help.

Brand new continental cars are a favourite target, although older cars are increasingly wanted, perhaps for the spare parts. Those which have foreign registration plates have a high

There is a rumour that if one buys car insurance from a certain company with connections to the mafia, no one would dare steal your car, although I cannot verify the truth.

risk of being stolen. Not parking your car in a dark, side street may lessen the risk of your car disappearing, but unfortunately, it´s no guarantee. The German-registered VW of someone we knew disappeared on his sixth day in the country, while parked in the street front of his office.

With the high incidence of car theft, most cars have alarms. These alarms go off whenever there is a fireworks display (weddings and opening ceremonies), a thunderstorm or when a heavy truck rolls by, rendering alarms so common that nobody pays any attention anymore.

The Traffic Police

If there´s anyone that strikes more fear in drivers´ hearts than manic drivers, then it´s the traffic policemen (KAT). They pull drivers over to check papers, check their cars and ask all sorts of questions. Out of town, they usually lurk behind bushes or round a corner to catch offenders. Bulgarians and foreigners alike will have incredible stories to tell you about the police, and they are unlikely to be exaggerated. If you are stopped by the police, try to remain calm and polite. The policemen are unlikely to be able to speak English. They have to find ways to supplement their miserable income. Spot fines for minor offences are common, and they sometimes ask for

The Police strikes terror in the hearts of most drivers, including law-abiding ones.

cash payment in dollars or Euros, and no prizes for guessing where the cash goes to. Some people say you should ask for a receipt before you hand over the cash. Others say you only make matters worse this way. Whatever your principles are about fighting corruption, you can´t really win this game.

The traffic police must be called (Tel:165) in the event of an accident, and an accident report filed. Few of the policemen speak English, so if you are not conversant in Bulgarian, it´s best to call a Bulgarian colleague/friend, or the car rental company.

Know Your Limits

Speed Limits: In the city: 50 km/hour; outside the city: 90 km/h; highways: 120 km/hour

Alcohol Limit: 0.5 /1000

Petrol and Car-Wash

It is recommended that you only use the reputable filling stations like OMV, Shell and BP for reliable quality of petrol. Petrol (92, 95 and 98 octanes), diesel and gas are available. The attendant will clean your windows apart from filling up your tank and would be grateful for a tip.

Some petrol stations have car-washing facilities. For 7 leva, your car gets washed, manually, while you wait with a coffee (included in the 7 leva), and for 4 leva, you can have it automatically done.

Strange Sounds and what they mean

- Sirens: At exactly 12 noon on 2 June, sirens will sound in all major cities for five minutes. Don´t be alarmed and think that Bulgaria is being invaded yet again; it´s just to commemorate those who died fighting to liberate Bulgaria from the Ottomans. Everyone stands still and observe 5 minutes of silence.
- Horning of cars-while mostly signifying the impatience of a driver, prolonged horning can mean there´s a wedding party driving along (especially on weekends), or high school kids celebrating their graduation (around second half of May).

Walking

In the city centre of Sofia, traffic hardly moves especially on workdays, so walking is often a better option. The problem is only that the pavements, like the roads, are usually in less than desirable condition. Metal grates over manholes and drains may be missing, uneven pavements and metal protusions gleefully trip you up, all just to create some excitement in the lives of pedestrians. Many shops are in the basement, so there are sudden flights of steps leading down to them along the pavement that pedestrians have to watch out for. But looking at the ground for all these potential traps may cause you to walk into a glass door of a street level shop, which is normally left open in summer, as the smaller

Missing drain covers and exposed metal stumps make walking a hazard for pedestrains on the streets of Sofia.

shops are not air-conditioned. But that´s presuming you are walking on the pavement at all; with the lack of parking spaces in the city centre, cars park on the pavements, forcing pedestrians to walk on the roads, instead. In May 2007, the Sofia municipality started erecting poles in some streets to prevent cars from parking up against the wall, so hopefully things will get better for pedestrians. What little amount of pavement left over for walking tends to be occupied by a group of people walking abreast deep in conversation with one another. Others stand there chatting and smoking, forcing you to walk on the road.

Crossing roads isn´t exactly easy either. At traffic lights, the ´green man´ comes on at the same time that turning traffic gets their ´green light´. Most Bulgarian drivers will charge round the corner and zoom past the pedestrians, except when there are young children around. It´s a question of crossing with determination, but not fighting with cars that seem even more determined than you. You learn to read the signs soon enough; but in the beginning, follow the locals. They have perfected the art of crossing roads. As a rough rule of thumb, you should not test your courage with delivery trucks, taxis and big expensive cars (especially those with darkened windows). At zebra crossings, don´t count on the worn-out black and white stripes painted on the roads. It´s best to wait until there are no cars before you try to cross the road.

When it rains, the poor drainage means puddles of water everywhere around which you have to negotiate to keep your shoes dry.

Motorcycles And Bicycles

Either one of these two options is practically suicidal, considering the road culture and conditions here. Bicycle lanes have recently been seen in Sofia, but hardly anyone cycles in the city centre, if they value their lives. So far, the users of bicycle lanes are mostly cars (parked on them), although six bicycle routes are planned for Sofia.

If you´re a cycling enthusiast, please have your fun off-road. *The Insider´s Guide* has great suggestions on where you can cycle safely around Sofia.

Public Transport

Bulgaria´s public transport system has seen little upgrading, so apart from the bright and clean central bus station in Sofia opened in 2004, the trains, buses and trams have seen better days.

Trains and Buses

Those looking at budget travel or adventure will find that taking the train and buses satisfies these wishes. Although very affordable, you will have to struggle with Cyrillic (except for international train services) and delays.

In Sofia, apart from buses, there are also trams and a single underground line running from Serdika station in the city centre to the western suburb of Lyulin. Be aware that pickpocketing happens frequently on buses. Women travelling alone overnight on trains might receive unwanted attention, sometimes including from train personnel.

Those intending to ride the trains and buses will find helpful tips in the *Rough Guide to Bulgaria* and *Sofia inyourpocket (please see Further Reading)*.

Taxis

Taxis are also very affordable (about 0.60 leva per km in the day, and slightly higher at night), until you get ripped off. Taxis at beach resorts may quote 2 Euros per km. There is no standardised rates; some taxi companies charge a much higher rate than others, so one has to scrutinise the rates displayed on the taxi. Although they are supposed to charge according to the meter, devious ones may switch off the meter or fiddle with it and charge you a rate fit for space tourism. Usually the taxis waiting outside hotels and major train stations are the worst vultures, especially when they see a foreigner.

In mid 2007 taxi services at Terminal Two of Sofia Airport was a traveller´s nightmare. A racket seemed to be going on at Arrivals; taxis demanded anything from 50 leva to 50 Euros for what should have cost only about 10 leva for a trip down to the city centre. After a huge outcry by tourists and expatriates, things have been ironed out. There is a taxi stand with OK taxis outside the Arrival Hall to your right as you come out from Baggage Claim. Avoid the touts waiting in the Arrival Hall.

There is an unofficial tradition for a price hike on New Year´s Eve. Flagging down a taxi on New Year´s Eve will be difficult; it´s better to book in advance.

To know whether a taxi is available or not when flagging one down on the streets, look for a small light on the front passenger side; green means it´s available and red means it´s occupied. Few speak a foreign language, and don´t count on taxi drivers knowing their way around. Many will blast your ear drums with loud music (one even had music downloaded from a memory stick!). Having lots of smaller 2 to 10 leva notes is advisable, as taxi drivers may say they have don´t have the change.

The average taxi is rather small, with a tiny boot (American: trunk), which is sometimes half taken up by a gas tank, so if you´re travelling with the entire family or lots of luggage, you might need to book two taxis.

Different cities have different taxi companies. In Sofia, OK and Yes are two of the more reputable companies. Booking a taxi is getting increasingly sophisticated. OK not only has English speaking operators, but now sends you the taxi number and estimated time of pick-up by SMS. Taxi drivers expect the fare to be rounded up, as a form of tipping.

Taxis waiting for passengers outside the Radisson SAS Grand Hotel, Sofia.

> **Taxi Companies in Sofia**
> - OK Supertrans   9732121
> - Radio CB Taxi   91263
> - Sofiataxi   9744747
> - Yes and Yellow   91119

Flying

Sofia Airport is Bulgaria´s main international airport, and since December 2006, there are two terminals. The airports in Varna and Bourgas are for domestic flights and in summer, receive international charter flights. Plovdiv Airport is basically for freight flights, and receives international charter flights only in winter. With the increase of tourism, it is expected that Varna, Bourgas and Plovdiv airports will take in lots more international flights all year round. A new terminal opened in Varna airport in mid June 2007.

SHOPPING
Supermarkets

Things have changed drastically compared to ten years ago. Expatriates who came to Bulgaria in the late 1990s had no access to imported goods, apart from two shops for which you needed a diplomatic pass to get in.

Today foreign chains like Metro, HIT, Billa and Kaufland are present in Bulgaria, with Carrefour, Plus and (Serbian) Delta M entering the market soon. The supermarkets are well-stocked with basic needs and don´t-needs ranging from food items, household items, to stationery and clothes. Most have bakeries within, where you can get freshly-baked bread.

Local chains like Picadilly, Fantastiko, Elemag and Familia are also very comprehensively stocked with both local and imported goods. Elemag, which started in 1998, used to be *the* place for more up-market groceries, before the arrival of the hypermarkets. It also has a gourmet restaurant.

The usual staples like fresh meat and fish, vegtables, fruits, Nestlé breakfast cereal of every kind, baby napkins (Huggies, Pampers) and baby food (Hipp and Nestlé) can all be found in the supermarkets. More exotic items like Asian food (sauces, noodles, tofu, fresh ginger) are also available in HIT, Picadilly and Elemag (all carrying a wide range of Thai sauces). The type of goods on offer increases all the time. By mid 2007, those pining for a real beef steak (and not the jaw-exercising *teleshko*) could get Argentinian steak.

At Picadilly, Billa and Fantastico supermarkets, you have to get your fruits and vegetables weighed and price-tagged (unless there's a price stated on the cling-wrapped item) before heading to the cashier. At HIT, this is done automatically at the cashier.

And yes, there is Heinz baked beans (some Brits say the Italian Victory brand is just as good) bacon and brown gravy sauce (local brand, not *Bisto*). No, there's no Marmite or Bovril, or Cheddar cheese, but a variety of hard yellow cheese, both local (*kashkaval*) and imported from other European countries.

Billa supermarkets also helpfully have pictures of a chicken, pig, cow etc at the the various meat counters to help `illiterate´ foreigners identify the type of meat on offer.

Don´t fight shy of some of the Bulgarian products; there are some good jams (e.g.Storko brand) and yoghurt and the cheeses are fine.

Picadilly has a wide range of very fresh fish, and not the almost mummified types which you sometimes come across in other supermarkets.

A note about buying vegetables that are pre-packed in styrofoam; sometimes the bottoms are already mouldy due to the condensation in the air-tight package.

Make sure you have stotinkis with you if you need a supermarket trolley. HIT supermarkets need a 20 or 50 stotinki slotted into the trolley, while Picadilly supermarkets need a 1 lev coin.

Outside most supermarkets are lockers where you are supposed to stow away your big bags. If you take your shopping bag into the supermarket, the security guards may want to check it when you come out. As there is a lot of counterfeit money going round, some supermarkets have scanners which the cashier will use to scan your money. They do it quite often, so don´t feel offended.

In their effort to go green, supermarket also charge 10 to 15 stotinki for each plastic bag you take. Picadilly supermarket started in early 2007 to sell canvas bags for 2.99 leva. Bringing your own shopping bag as your contribution to saving the earth usually only gets puzzled looks from cashiers. I had a feeling they often thought I was too poor or stingy to pay a few stotinki for a plastic bag.

Most of the supermarkets have very long opening hours, and stay open through the weekends and public holidays, including important ones like Easter, a real treat for many West Europeans.

Open Markets

The best place to get the freshest fruits and vegetables and the incredibly good Bulgarian honey is the open market. The prices are often displayed, and many of them have scales which indicate the price you have to pay, so you don´t have to worry too much about your inability to speak Bulgarian.

One problem is that some stall holders will not let you pick the fruits or vegetables yourself; so you may find that the tomatoes that looked so good on display are rotten on the underside when you get home. If any stallholder refuses to let you select your own apples or tomatoes, you can always go to another stall.

The range and quality of honey are delightful. Many of them are bottled in recycled jars, which lend them a home-made feel. If you´re an eco-friendly type, the recyled jars are another plus on top of the affordable price (about 8 leva a kg).

In Sofia, the Zhenski Pazar (Women´s market) is one of the best known. Located at Stefan Stambolov Boulevard, near the synagogue and mosque, this market sells vegetables, fruits, honey, flowers, cheap clothes, household goods and even things you would not expect to find in a market. Even if you´re not buying anything in particular, the hustle and bustle is something a foreigner should experience at least once. Just look out for the pickpockets, though. Other markets can be found at Shipchenski Prohod Boulevard (near the Romanian Embassy), Graf Ignatiev (near the Sveti Sedmochislentsi church), Hristo Smirnenski Boulevard, opposite the architecture school and on Petko Todorov Boulevard, near the Rakovski sports complex. The latter is also accessible from Kraishte Street, just off the Yuzhen Park end of Vitosha Boulevard.

At the market on Hristo Smirnenski Boulevard, you can even combine marketing with a spot of archaeology. This small market is called Rimska Stena (Roman Wall) Market precisely because there is really such a piece of preserved wall standing there.

Techno Markets

An extensive range of electronic goods can be found in the technomarkets. These can be found in the Mall of Sofia, City Centre Sofia, HIT supermarket, and just behind TZUM.

Shopping Malls

Shopping malls are appearing fast and furious in major cities. Three large shopping malls already exist in Sofia, with many more expected. The Mall of Sofia (35,000 sq.m/376.737 sq. ft), City Center Sofia (approx. 20,000 sq.m/215,278 sq. ft) and Sky City Center (approx. 26,000 sq. m/279,862 sq. ft) offer a wide range of retail therapists. International clothes brands like Guy Larouche, French Connection, Marks and Spencers and Calvin Klein, supermarkets, electronic goods shops, bookshops and chic cafes occupy these temples of consumerism.

While most five star hotels have souvenir shops, the range may not be very wide and the prices are often higher than the average. Souvenirs can be found at the Centre of Folk Arts & Crafts in the former Tsar´s Palace on Battenberg Square, or at Traditzia at 38, Vassil Levski Boulevard (near 6 Septembri street). Traditzia is a charity gift shop with most of the products produced by disadvantaged members of society.

Those who find cookie-cutter type of shopping malls lacking in local flavour may prefer to amble round the traditional shopping areas before the arrival of shopping malls. In Sofia, Vitosha Boulevard is the Oxford Street of Sofia. Shops carrying international brand names like Joop!, Tommy Hilfiger and United Colours of Benetton can be found here as well as local retailers. The boulevard is closed to traffic, except for the tram and traffic flowing at right angles to it. The side streets branching out from Vitosha Boulevard, and indeed, all the side streets around the city centre are worth trawling, to give you a feel of the `real´ Sofia. Tsar Ivan Shishman Street, Graf Ignatiev Street, Shipka Street, and Pirotska Street, to name a few, are home to an eclectic range of galleries, bookshops, gift shops, shoe shops, fruit and vegetable stalls and lingerie shops. The number of quality lingerie shops to be found in the city centre is amazing. Some of them have names like Libido and the enigmatic Seven Seconds. I´m still trying to figure out seven seconds to what? One thing which women with larger frames have noticed is that the sizes of clothes in the local shops seem made for our teenage daughters.

Fans of TCM products carried by the Tchibo coffee chain can also be found in little TCM outlets around Sofia (e.g. on Maria Luisa Boulevard close to Pop Bogomil Street). These shops carry old stocks and not the latest products that come out weekly in Germany and the UK. Loyal consumers of Spanish chain Zara can find older collections (and at lower prices) of Zara apparel in Z outlets in Sofia (off Vitosha Boulevard just next to Pizza Palace, Bulgaria Boulevard 88 and in Sky City Shopping Centre in the district of Geo Milev) and in Varna. By the time you read this, the planned outlets in Plovdiv, Blagoevgrad, Burgas, Veliko Turnovo, Pleven, Sandanski and Sunny Beach are probably already opened too.

One unusual feature you will find in Sofia is the basement shops. The vendors sell their drinks and snacks from the shop window located more or less at feet level of the pedestrians. Customers have to squat or bend their backs to select their purchases. The other unusual, somewhat heart-breaking, sight are the pet shops which boast their wares in the shop windows. You may chance upon shops where puppies gaze forlornly at you with their melting brown eyes.

Two grand dames of Sofia are a must for foreigners: TZUM Shopping Centre (an acronym for the Bulgarian name Tzentralen Universalen Magazin) and Halite covered market. TZUM (at 2 Maria Luisa Boulevard, near the Sheraton Hotel) used to be *the* department store in Sofia and is worth a visit for its historical significance. It's the Bulgarian Harrods, put simply. TZUM is not exactly exciting for the younger generation, who prefer to throng the newer malls, hence the TZUM management decided to liven things up by bringing in an eight-month-old Siberian tiger, Shakti, in Nov 2006. Born in a Czech zoo, she was put in a glass cage on the third floor of TZUM, much to the chagrin of animal lovers.

Halite is an enormous former covered food market at the corner of Pirotska Street and Vitosha Boulevard. There is a food court and a number of small shops on the upper level, and stalls selling honey, fish, fruits and vegetables on the ground floor. Like TZUM, the building and its history make it attractive.

Daylight Saving Time

Bulgaria observes daylight saving time; at the end of March, the clock advances by one hour (i.e. from 11pm to midnight) and at the end of October, it moves back one hour (i.e. from midnight to 11 pm).

Special Dietary Needs-Vegans; Halal Food, Kosher Food

Lacto-ovo vegetarians have a fairly good choice from Bulgarian cuisine; delicious salads, non-meat starters and soups. For home cooking, there are also plenty of fresh fruits and vegetables, nuts, beans, cereals, yoghurt and cheese (made from either cow's, sheep's, goat's or buffalo's milk). In Sofia,

Basement shops are a unique
feature of Sofia's shopping scene.

two restaurants for vegetarians to note are the Vegetarianskata Kashta, the Veggie Home (10 Patriarch Evtimi Boulevard) and Kibea health food restaurant (2A Dr. G. Valkovich).

Although there is a significant Muslim community in Bulgaria, most of them are not particular about eating only halal food, especially so in the case of the younger generation living in the cities. In the Muslim strongholds such as around Shumen and Razgrad in the north and Haskovo and Kurdzhali, the people may be more observant, but it is not easy to find halal food in other cities. In Sofia, the Turkish supermarket, Ramstore, may provide the answer. For eating out, Awadh Indian restaurant serves halal food.

Kosher food is also hard to come by. The Jewish Community Center at 50 Stamboliiski Street has a kosher restaurant. Kosher food is also available at the Sofia Hilton Hotel and Awadh Indian Restaurant.

DIY Stores

Mr. Bricolage (in Sofia, Bourgas and Plovdiv) and Praktiker (in Sofia, Varna, Plovdiv, Pleven and Veliko Turnovo) have enormous stores filled with all the basic equipment for much-needed home improvement or simply satisfying the urges of compulsive DIY-ers.

For The Myopic

There are modern optical shops in the cities with fahionable frames and other eye-care needs. For contact lens wearers, three-in-one solutions, especially OPTI-free, are widely available in pharmacies and optical shops. For solutions containing hydrogen peroxide (such as AO Sept), head for the optical shops instead.

Delivery Service

Lucky Sofianites now can rely on BGMENU, a delivery service offered by Road Runner SP Ltd. The products/services on offer include food, alcoholic drinks, groceries from Piccadilly and laundry services. The company takes orders through the phone, email or via their web page at http://www.bgmenu.com

HEALTH MATTERS
Vaccinations

There are no vaccination requirements for entry to Bulgaria, but if you will be living there for some time, about seven months before your departure, do check with your health care provider on the vaccinations you might need for your own protection; as some vaccinations (e.g. against hepatitis) need to be taken in a series spread over six months. Depending on where you intend to live and your personal risk factors, the vaccinations recommended to you may be against the following:

- Hepatitis A
- Hepatitis B
- Rabies
- Tick-borne encephalitis
- Tetanus

Although the probability of being bitten by ticks is not high, precaution is recommended because of the disease they transmit. When walking in rural fields, take precautions against ticks by wearing long trousers and tucking them into your socks and spraying skin and clothing with an insect repellant based on DEET (an abbreviation for a chemical with a mind-boggling name). For an even better protection, impregnate cotton clothing with permethrine. It's advisable to check your body thoroughly for ticks after a trip out in the wilds, as the sooner ticks are removed, the lesser the chance of being infected. Ticks are best removed with special tick tweezers, or see a doctor immediately if you´re unsure how to remove them. Pouring medicated oil or petrol is not advisable as it may make things worse. Avian flu H5N1 has been confirmed in Bulgaria, but only in migratory birds, and not in poultry. The risk of contracting avian flu is not high for those who don't work with birds, which means most of us. There is rabies in Bulgaria, but the incidents reported were mainly in the countryside. Still, getting vaccinated will give you peace of mind.

Water

Tap water is safe to drink, but for all new arrivals, it´s always best to stick to bottled water, which are readily available and is extremely cheap at about 90 stotinki for a 1.5l bottle.

Medical Services

The public health infrastructure in Bulgaria is not of a standard that people from developed countries are used to. The doctors are competent, but they are let down by the crumbling infrastructure. In the public hospitals, there is often one bathroom for the patients of an entire floor, and patients may have to bring their own dressing, bandages and even toilet paper. Nurses will not bring patients the bedpan unless they are paid each time they bring it. However, many of the private hospitals and clinics have good facilities and well-trained doctors who speak foreign languages such as English, German or French. Some embassies have appointed them as embassy doctors e.g. the German Embassy has a Bulgarian doctor manning a consultation room in a wing of the embassy building and his wife runs the Robert Koch Medical Centre, a facility which is of a more modest scale than its name suggests, but reassuringly clean and modern.

Cash is King
It's advisable to have enough cash on hand at home. Doctors and hospitals usually wish to be paid in cash.

Medical costs in Bulgaria is still significantly lower than in many developed countries, so medical tourism is picking up in Bulgaria. There are also many dentistries providing competent dental care.

For those who still feel most comfortable with the medical facilities at home, a comprehensive insurance which includes evacuation services would be worth looking into before coming.

PSYCHOLOGICAL HEALTH
Culture Shock

Many expatriates tend to underestimate culture shock, especially when they go to a country where the culture seems deceptively similar to theirs. But people do things differently in different countries, sometimes even in different regions within a country, so there will always be something or other that will come as a surprise to expatriates. The sense of disorientation that comes with being in an unfamiliar environment can affect different people in different degrees, at different times and in any country. First-time as well as seasoned expatriates can suffer from culture shock.

The people in the high-risk groups are the accompanying spouses and children. Often, the spouse has to forgo her (it's usually the wife who is the accompanying person) own career to accompany the husband on the posting, while the children leave their friends behind, to land in totally new surroundings. The slight advantage the husband has is that he's got his job as a focal point and colleagues to ask for information, things which his accompanying family does not have. The feeling of disorientation is therefore often more acutely felt by the accompanying family.

A *Sofia Echo* journalist interviewed expatriate teenagers in Sofia, and the most common things they missed most were friends, shopping (although a lot of shopping malls have sprung up since then), family, the way of life in their home countries and marshmallows, Dr. Pepper and Taco Bell. The common shock faced by expatriate wives I've met is the loss of identity-reduced to being known only as `Mr. Johnson's wife´ or `Sarah's mom´. Coming to Bulgaria also presents an additional challenge of having to grapple with a new alphabet, Cyrillic.

If you suddenly feel you've become excessively irritable or insecure, lethargic and in need of a lot of sleep, or feel unsociable and prefer to stay at home, find everything about the host country unbearable or cry over the smallest things, then chances are you're encountering culture shock.

Different people have different ways of combating culture shock. Cross-cultural experts recommend that you go out and make friends with other expatriates and locals, find something concrete to do in the form of a job or charity work, learn more about your host country and focusing on the positive things that the posting has to offer. What's important is to understand that suffering from culture shock is not something to be ashamed of, but rather like having the flu; you feel lousy, but once you recognise the ailment, you know it's not life-threatening and you can do something to get better. Being a foreigner is exactly that; things *are* foreign to you so there's no need to be perfect in everything you do.

If you make a mistake, or get cheated by the taxi, shrug it off as part of the learning process. Don´t let the passing phase of confusion shatter your self-confidence and identity.

And celebrate the fact that you´re coming at a good time; expatriates who came to Bulgaria as recent as five years ago had a much harder time. Some other countries are even more challenging too.

Winter Blues and Seasonal Affective Disorder

Dark and cold winters, such as those in Bulgaria, can affect people in an unpleasant way.

Researchers have concluded that the lack of sunlight in the fall and winter causes seasonal depression. The darker days results in the brain not producing enough serotonin, which results in the symptoms of depression, while overproducing a sleep hormone, melatonin. That can leave a person feeling down and lethargic (winter blues), or in more serious cases, with impaired social interaction and cognitive ability (Seasonal Affective Disorder).

Winter blues and Seasonal Affective Disorder can be treated with light therapy. Ordinary household lighting is not enough to reverse seasonal depression, but specialised bright light (of 10,000 lux intensity or more) works wonders. It´s best to consult a physician, but be reassured that such lamps are available for use at home, although so far I´ve not come across any in Bulgaria.

Exercise, even if it´s only a half-hour brisk walk outdoors, is also said to be helpful. If for any reason you are unable to go outdoors, sitting at an open window (wrapped up warmly, of course) for about 20 minutes will also give you a dose of the lux out there.

TELECOMMUNICATIONS
Telephones and Internet

Bulgaria´s telephone system has been undergoing digitisation and modernisation, with priority given to business communications. Many companies offer entire packages for telephone and internet connection. Both dial-up and broadband internet connection are available, for very reasonable prices. A broadband connection costs about 30 to 40 Leva per month for unlimited access. There are also internet cafes in the major cities and tourist resorts, although Bulgarians mainly use them for computer games.

The connection in Sofia is reliable and the server is very rarely down. If you find that you are not getting a connection, unplug the connection cable or switch off the modem and reconnect/switch on the modem after 30 seconds. Usually the connection will come on. If this doesn´t work, then the server is down, which usually lasts for a few hours. When that happens, it could be a fault at the end of the internet provider, or you have inadvertently forgotten to pay your subscriptions.

Most public phones in Bulgaria are now worked by phone cards, which can be purchased from kiosks and post offices. Some phones still accept coins, but most are out of order due to vandalism. Local and long-distance calls to Europe can be made from Betkom and Bulfon phone booths with Betkom or Bulfon phone cards respectively. Calls can also be made at post offices, where cash can be used instead of phone cards. Mobile phones can be used almost everywhere in Bulgaria, except for some remote areas in the mountains. Most mobile phones will roam here in Bulgaria, but as roaming charges are exorbitant, it's preferable to buy a local SIM card from any one of the GSM operators. Both subscription and pre-paid cards are available.

One thing to note is that some network operators 'lock' their mobile phones so that you are restricted to using only their network. If your existing phone is locked, you cannot use a SIM card supplied by another network provider unless you get your phone unlocked by the original network provider, for a fee.

Your phone must also be a GSM compatible (as opposed to CDMA compatible) to be able to use the Bulgarian SIM cards, unless you have one of those super dual network type of phones.

All in all, the telecommunications companies are efficient with up-to-date technology, including payment modes (direct debit from bank accounts and ATM, phone and Internet payments).

BANKING

Bulgaria´s banking system has come a long way since 1996 when it tethered on the edge of collapse. Foreign banks, both full banks and branches are operating in Bulgaria. Foreign banks in Bulgaria include BNP-Paribas, Citibank, Raiffeisen Bank and ING Bank.

There are many ATM machines in Sofia and the bigger cities, where you can also use your foreign bank card or credit card to draw cash, usually for a hefty fee charged by your bank or credit card company. The ATMs run out of cash very quickly during the Christmas and New Year holiday season, so you may wish to withdraw sufficient cash before that. The limit on the amount available for withdrawal per day may be very low (my bank's limit is 400 leva). If you need cash to pay your rent (very often the case), you have to squirrel away 400 leva in stages, or go to the bank to withdraw the total sum.

Opening an account in a bank in Bulgaria is not hard. Most banks have staff who speak fluent English. You will need to have a permanent address in Bulgaria to open an account.

Do check if the account pays interest, if there´s a fee for holding that account, if they charge exorbitant rates for receipt of foreign currency by electronic transfer into your own account or for (this is a real injustice) withdrawing your own money and the minimum amount needed to open an account. Some banks also offer internet banking, which can save you a lot of time. However, make sure the bank has in place sophisticated security to minimise internet fraud.

Changing Money
Never change money with strangers on the streets. Go to a bank or exchange bureau

Credit Cards

Credit cards are accepted in most establishments in the major cities, although not as wildly popular as say, in North America. As mentioned above, they can be used to withdraw cash from ATM machines. You will need your pin number.

POSTAL SERVICES AND CUSTOMS OFFICE

Post offices can be found in cities and villages, and the postal system is reasonably efficient. Ordinary mail to and from

Europe takes about a week, and to North America and Asia Pacific, between two to three weeks.

For foreigners, the challenge is trying to figure out correctly which counter to go to, to post letters or buy stamps, as you are not likely to find an English-speaking postal worker. Joining at random a queue of people may well land you in the one meant for pensioners collecting their monthly allowances.

Sending parcels will require that you bring your stuff unwrapped to the central (not any neighbourhood) post office and fill up a customs declaration before wrapping up your parcel. Heavy parcels have to be collected from a special customs office.

Some people have complained of not receiving letters. They suspect that the envelope may have been opened to see if there's cash within, and the letter simply thrown away, whether or not the cash search yielded positive results. At the special customs office where one collects heavier parcels, an officer was seen rifling through a box and helping herself to a handful of pens from the box and putting them aside before re-sealing the box. Presumably, the pens were not taken out to be sent to a laboratory for special testing. Others have had to wait for an eternity to get an equipment replacement part through customs, and asked to pay such a hefty price for release of the piece that it was a better option in the end to put an employee on a plane to pick up the piece personally from overseas.

Addressing Mail

If you want to be very correct, addressing mail to Bulgaria should be in this sequence:

1421 Sofia

Boulevard Arsenalski 123, Apt 11

Mr Georgi Vassilev

But even if you address it the 'usual' way of recipient's name first, followed by street and apartment and lastly postcode and city, the post will still reach you. As a matter of fact, I find the Bulgarian sequence a lot more logical.

PUBLIC TOILETS

If you are the sort who needs to take a leak often, public facilities out of the cities will be a hit and miss. In the countryside, I've seen both basic but clean lavatories and really primitive ones. They can come with seats or be mere holes in the ground. Toilet paper may or may not be available, so it´s best to have your own tissue paper with you every time you visit one plus some coins as they often charge for usage. You may sometimes see a wastepaper basket or bin where you're supposed to put your paper in instead of down the hole, as the flushing system is not exactly efficient. In some places, there are no separate areas for men and women, so it's quite awkward to have to walk into a room with men in it, although there are separate cubicles.

If there are separate male and female lavatories, these may sometimes be indicated only with Cyrillic alphabets, without any male or female figures plastered on the doors. 'М' is the men's department and `Ж´ or `Д´ refers to the ladies.

In Sofia itself, clean facilities can be found in shopping centres, the underpass near the Presidency and in most restaurants.

In the more working class parks, you may sometimes spot adults doing their thing in a not too bushy part of the park. With children, there's even less modesty; mothers just pull down the kids' pants and let them pee in the open. On the highways, you sometimes see men taking the pressure off their bladders standing next to their cars right there on the shoulders of the highways.

DISPOSING OF RUBBISH

Bagged rubbish must be brought to the dumpsters lined along the streets. In residential areas in Sofia, there is one every 100 to 200 metres. As of 2007, Sofia is also full of recycling bins. These are a trio of blue, yellow and green (for paper, plastic and glass respectively) bins, as opposed to the general rubbish bins which are of plain steel. Enthusiastic environmentalists dutifully separated their rubbish and popped them into the different bins, only to find out in April 2007 that one of the contractors collected the separated rubbish and dumped them all into the single compartment of the collecting truck. Back to square one.

Although these colourful recycling bins are new, recycling itself is a much older tradition, although the motivation was necessity rather than environmental protection. The Roma people, and sadly, increasingly more elderly people, pick through the dumpsters to salvage whatever they can for re-use or sale, such as old jam jars, plastic bottles and leftover food.

Rubbish may not be something that is newsworthy, but in Sofia and its environs, it is a major issue. After years of neglect, Sofia's waste disposal problem came to a head in 2005 when the city's main refuse site in Suhodol was closed after the residents there blocked the road, saying that Sofia's mayor had promised its closure in 2005. A decision was then made to build a refuse processing plant, but since that would take at least a year, a solution had to be found for the refuse in the interim period. The rubbish were baled, and left in several small sites, but soon these sites bcame over-crowded. The new mayor, Boiko Borissov, who had plans to enter politics, was particularly passionate about the rubbish problem, and even threatened to dump the rubbish in front of government offices if they did not help resolve the issue.

Eventually, a deal between Sofia and Plovdiv was signed, whereby Sofia could transport 200,000 tons of garbage to a landfill in Tsalapitsa, near Plovdiv, with the government promising to allot 47 million leva to Plovdiv for building of infrastructure for its help. The village of Tsalapitsa itself was to receive 3 million leva to improve their infrastructure. So those using the highway from Sofia to Plovdiv will see trucks with plastic-wrapped bales of compressed rubbish on their way to Tsalapitsa.

BEGGARS

Thankfully, one isn't persistently swarmed by young begging children tugging and pulling at your clothes, or by deformed beggars aggressively sticking their hands through the car window while you are stuck in a traffic jam. It may be hard

The elderly often set up make-shift stalls to sell sweets or other sundry items to earn some money.

50 CT

to ignore the handicapped person hobbling among the cars, walk past an elderly person or a bedraggled child asking for a few stotinki, but be aware that there are begging syndicates around, using in particular, Roma children for begging and washing of car windows. To avoid giving money to syndicate heads who are milking the elderly or young children, but at the same time not be plagued by guilt for being hard-hearted, buy nuts, herbs or sweets from the elderly vendors. These hard-working pensioners are trying to keep a modicum of respect by selling something, instead of begging, and will need every lev they can get. Giving sweets and biscuits instead of money to the beggar children is more likely to benefit them directly instead of the person who is exploiting them.

Another way to help the needy without worrying that it lands in the wrong hands would be to buy handicraft from charity galleries, such as Traditzia.

It's difficult, if not impossible, to know whether a beggar is part of a syndicate or not. There are enough poor people around who genuinely need help and it certainly doesn't hurt those of us who can afford to part with a lev or two to give to a beggar, without a prior Sherlock Holmes check.

STRAY DOGS

Stray dogs on the streets are generally not aggressive, but there have been some nasty incidents. In January 2005, 10 stray dogs attacked a 34 year-old jogger in the city centre of Sofia. She was certainly not the first victim, only that the 109 bites she suffered brought the problem to public attention. Others have reported having to negotiate their way between packs of snarling dogs at night.

Even if not dangerous, they are a nuisance, as they spend the days sleeping soundly in the parks and streets to be sufficiently refreshed to spend the nights barking to wake us up. Ear plugs are a possible solution.

Sofianites have an aversion to sterilisation, not to speak of euthanasia, so the problem looks likely to remain for the time being.

NOISE

Car horns blaring, car alarms going off for no apparent
reason, endless construction work going on and dogs
barking, the bigger cities, especially Sofia are certainly
not places that know the word 'quiet'. For that, you have
to run off to the mountains. The Bulgarians are so used to
noise that no one seems to complain about the noise the
neighbours make. Our neighbour immediately above our
flat had kids that screamed, cried and/or trampled right
up to 1:00 am. Often the mother adds to the cacophony
by screaming at her kids. Another had a big baritone dog
which would test out its vocal chords in the early hours of
the morning. Some days, protests or other events would
take place in the park nearby, with people shouting into the
loudspeakers and music blaring. Noise is something which
you just have to get used to.

FOOD & DRINK

CHAPTER 6

'I want the Scots to drink Rakia.'
—Georgi Purvanov, President of Bulgaria,
during his campaign for a second term in the presidency,
shortly before the country joined the European Union.

As a result of its geographic location and history, Bulgarian cuisine has a heavy Slavonic, Turkish and Greek influence, tempered by European modifications. Those pining for Turkish and Greek familiar favourites like stuffed vine leaves, *moussaka*, *kofta/keftedes*, *raki/ouzo* will find that these have Bulgarian cousins. The Turkish/Greek influences join hands with the Bulgarian countryside-staples to produce a hearty cuisine, washed down with a good selection of Bulgarian libation.

Bulgarian cuisine uses a lot of vegetables (in salads, stews or just roasted). The most common ones are cucumbers, tomatoes (actually a fruit), peppers, carrots, eggplants, cabbage and leeks.

Market stalls offer a good variety of fresh fruit and vegetables as these ingredients feature prominently in Bulgarian cuisine.

Halite is one of the places where one is able to find a selection of meats and innards for sale.

Chicken and pork are the two most common meats. Beef is less common, but available, and commonly referred to as veal, although you´d be suprised how un-veal like it tastes. Rather, it tends to be like eating a piece of leather, although in some better restaurants, the beef is fine. The Bulgarian beef is a reflection of the fact that it has been more a by-product of milk production, rather than cattle bred for the meat itself. Fish is also not popular, except in the coastal regions, and when it has to be eaten on St. Nicholas Day (6 December). In spring, lamb is extremely popular, especially at Easter. Rabbits, wild boar, venison, chicken hearts and livers are also eaten. Westerners often cringe at what they find in some markets (e.g. Halite), such as whole heads of pigs or sheep, actually smiling contentedly, or pig trotters, ears and other innards. If you´re adventurous, chicken hearts and livers taste good. Besides, eating innards isn´t exactly such a novelty; after all, sausage skins are intestines and pate and foie gras are essentially liver.

Yoghurt and white cheese also have a starring role in Bulgarian cuisine.

Bulgarians like their food well spiced and seasoned, and are often enhanced with herbs like savory (*Chubritsa*), dill, mint, paprika, basil and allspice.

Bread is a staple in Bulgaria and accompanies all meals. While the bread offered in the average restaurant may be uninspiring, home-made bread is unbeatable. Supermarkets also offer a wide range of breads, from the darker German variety to sliced toast which the British folks can put their beloved Heinz baked beans (also available in Bulgarian supermarkets) on.

No self-respecting Bulgarian passes up on libation of some sort during a meal, with *rakia* and Bulgarian wine being the most common drinks to wash down the food..

FOOD
Fruits And Vegetables

About 30 per cent of Bulgaria is arable land, so there is a regular supply of fresh seasonal fruits and vegetables. From the popular food items, you can deduce the types of crops the country has. Spinach, nettles and young garlic in spring, all types of berries, watermelons, tomatoes and cucumbers in late spring and summer, pumpkins (just in time for Halloween) in autumn and gherkins in winter guarantee a very varied menu in Bulgaria. Bananas (from Ecuador and other neighbours) are available all year round. You will notice that very oxidised bananas (all brown and squishy) are still sold (and bought!). Of course, some buy them because they are much cheaper in this sorry state, but the older Bulgarians don't bat an eyelid probably because they're used to seeing bananas in this condition during the earlier difficult years (when bananas were available at all).

The fruits and vegetables that come from the gardens and small plots of land in the villages are organic, for the simple reason that the farmers cannot afford pesticides or other chemicals. I've sometimes found a wriggling worm or two in my spinach or berries; a sure sign that they're organic, unless someone has popped the critters in there to fool me. Bulgaria does have organic farms, growing berries, herbs and mushrooms, but they are mainly for export. Spinach and potatoes also tend to come with the dirt still clinging to them, probably to add a few grams to the total weight.

There is nowadays a wide range of exotic imported fruits and vegetables such as pineapples, lychees (often looking exhausted from their arduous journey), mangoes, kiwis, baby carrots, baby asparagus and baby corn etc coming from far away Latin American countries and South Africa.

Dairy Products

At the time that Bulgaria joined the European Union in January 2007, there were more than 300 Bulgarian companies producing dairy products. Many brands of milk, yoghurt and cheese are available.

It is widely believed that yoghurt originated in Bulgaria and as long ago as during the times of the Thracians, when it was `discovered´ that the milk carried in the lambskin bags became fermented by the warmth of the bodies. Called *kiselo mlyako* (sour milk), there is also one brand that is organically produced, called Bio. If you're lucky enough to get home-made yoghurt, then it's the ultimate of Bulgarian yoghurt. At risk of sounding like Prince Charles, the home-made yoghurt probably tastes better because it's made from raw (unpasteurised and failing EU minimum health standards) milk. Bulgarian yoghurt is popular as far away as Japan, where Meiji Dairies produces a total of 200,000 tons of Bulgarian yoghurt annually. *Ayran*, a popular drink especially in summer, is basically yoghurt with water added.

Cheeses are the feta-like white cheese, *sirene*, or the hard yellow *kashkaval* (like cheddar cheese). Some of the *sirene* come coated with herbs.

The yoghurt and cheese are made from cow's, sheep's, goat's or buffalo's milk. Lactose intolerant types can depend on the non-cow version of cheese and yoghurt.

As at the beginning of 2007, only 30 of the 300 dairy products companies had the green light to sell to the European market.

Herbs and Other Plants

Bulgaria is blessed with about 3,000 different types of plants growing in the mountain areas. About 300 species are used in the pharmaceutical industries, and 750 as alternative medicines. Popular herbs include mint, lavender, wild marjoram, dill, thyme, St. John's Wort, savory (*chubritsa*) and sage. Bulgaria exports about 12,000 tons of medicinal herbs per year, mostly to Europe and the United States. The herbs are also widely used as tea and to season food.

Herb gathering has a long tradition in Bulgaria. Very often you see Bulgarians wandering around the mountains with plastic bags in hand, picking herbs for their own use.

Bulgaria is also famous for its rose oil. The Bulgarian Rosa Damascena, cultivated for over 300 years, is considered to be a premium oil-producing variety.

It is the world's second largest producer of rose oil, an important component of perfume. The rose oil is mainly exported to France, Germany and the United States. The Valley of the Roses to the south of the Balkan range is the hub of rose oil production. Some 3,000 kilos of rose petals are needed for a litre of rose oil. The next time you pick up a bottle of Chanel or Calvin Klein, just note that it might have an ingredient from Bulgaria.

Other plants like nettle are used for salads and soups, and the rose hip are used for teas or jams.

Bulgarian Honey

Honey gathering is also an old Bulgarian tradition, said to be practised by the Slavic tribes in the Bulgarian lands as

Different varieties of honey for sale; Bulgaria exports most of her output to countries within the European community.

early as 7 AD. when it was gathered for its nutritional and medicinal uses. Bulgaria's abundant nature is conducive for honey production. The wide variety of plants and trees ensures different types of flavours. Bulgaria produces about 9,600 tons of honey per year. Most of this is exported to the European Union.

St. Haralampi, the Orthodox patron saint of bee-keepers, is remembered on 10 February. The saint is believed to have been the first to discover the healing powers of honey.

If the honey becomes too crystallised for your liking (which happens often in winter when it's cold), just stand the jar in warm water and the honey will become a creamy consistency again.

One of the delicacies that should not be missed when in Bulgaria are the many varieties of salami and sausages.

Bulgarian Salami And Sausages

Bulgaria also has a wide selection of salami, made from pork, deer meat, buffalo meat or even ostrich, and often mixed with herbs and spices. The area around Bansko is famed for its sausages, including the much lauded *Banski Starets*.

BULGARIAN LIBATION

Unlike the Germans (who are usually associated with beer), or the French (synonymous with wine), Bulgarians embrace their spirits, wines and beers with the same loving intensity.

Spirits

When the president of Bulgaria, Georgi Purvanov, said he wanted the Scots to drink *rakia*, he wasn´t exactly joking. The Bulgarians are proud and fond of their *rakia*, a brandy usually made from plums, apricots or grapes (respectively *slivova, kaisieva* and *grozdova/muskatova*). *Mastika* is another favourite, which is made from aniseed (basically like the Greek *ouzo*). *Pliska*, a cognac, is also popular.

Spirits are never drunk on their own; they are accompanied by a soft drink, and a salad or appetizer. At the very least, one must drink spirits with some nibbles like sausages and olives. Bulgarians will think you extremely odd if you don´t.

Wines

Oenophiles have a wide selection to choose from in Bulgaria. Bulgarian wine, especially the red wine, is exported to more than 70 countries with Great Britain, Germany and Russia at the top of the list of export countries. There are some 3,000 vine varieties, including the internationally-known reds like *cabernet sauvignon, pinot noir* and *merlot* and local grapes like *gumza, melnik* and *mavrud*. There are also white wines, like *chardonnay, misket* and *dimiat*, but the general agreement is that the reds are better.

Wine-making in Bulgaria is an ancient tradition, and said to go back to the days of the Thracians. On 14 February, Bulgarians celebrate a Vine Grower´s Day as much (perhaps even more than) as they do Valentine´s Day.

Wine is very affordable, and ordering by the glass is never an issue in this country.

Beer

The market leaders are Zagorka, Carlsberg Bulgaria and Kamenitza (owned by international beer titans Heineken, Carlsberg and InBev respectively). In January 2007 alone, Zagorka sold 74,000 hectolitres of beer.

Enjoy the refreshing taste of Zagorka, one of the most popular beer that is brewed locally.

Bulgarians certainly like beer, proven by the fact that it has the highest consumption of Beck´s per capita in the world. A lot of the beer is sold in 2.5 litre PET (polyethelene terephthalate) bottles, those hardy plastic containers, which encourages high volume sales.

Heineken´s beer-dispensing device, the Beer Tender, (the espresso machine-like thing) is also available here.

OTHER BULGARIAN DRINKS
Boza
This is a fermented beverage, made from millet, wheat, maize or some other cereal and are sold in plastic bottles. It looks like chocolate milk-shake, but doesn´t taste anything like it.

Many people have tried to describe its taste, from a polite `an acquired taste´, to graphic `mushed-up Quaker Puffed Wheat´ to `the liquid that´s on the top when you open a can of kidney beans´. It has been mistakenly called a beer, probably because of the slight alcoholic content (1 to 4 per cent) due to fermentation, but it is regarded as a health drink in the region, rather than as an alcoholic drink.

Boza enjoyed its golden age during the Ottoman Empire, as the beverage was spread to all the occupied lands. It is currently enjoying a new fame with Europeans as a bust-booster, with A-cup sizers downing litres of the stuff in the hope of becoming a D-cup size overnight. When Bulgaria and Romania became EU members in January 2007, it was reported that Romanians poured across the border to Rousse (the Bulgarian town at the border) to snap up the magic potion. European men were also said to be rushing to buy the beverage for their girlfriends and wives.

Traditionally, it has been touted as having an ability to augment the milk production of lactating women. The medical explanation could be that *boza* raises the prolaction hormones that help milk production, and perhaps leading to breasts enlarging.

Boza is a beverage that is said to be able to help boost bustlines. It is best enjoyed with *banitsa*, a pastry snack.

Whatever you believe, *boza* producers are certainly enjoying a hey-day perhaps not seen since the Ottoman times, after international news media picked up on this piece of interesting news.

Mineral Water

Bulgaria has more than 500 mineral springs, with diverse chemical composition, temperatures and healing features.

Among the many different brands, Devin, Gorna Banya and Bankya are the well established ones. Mineral water are either still or carbonated (*gazyrana*). Bottle sizes start from a mini 330 ml bottle to a supersize 11 litres.

Bulgarians believe firmly in the curative powers of their mineral water, with different types of mineral water good for ailments affecting different bodily organs, hence the springs are not only a source of drinking water, but popular spas as well.

Coffee, Tea and Chocolate

Bulgarians prefer coffee over tea, so your chances of finding a good coffee is higher than a good tea. It´s very common to see Bulgarians walking around with a small disposable cup of coffee.

But the supermarkets carry imported teas (such as Twinings) as well as Bulgarian herbal teas (which the locals drink for curative reasons) and chinese tea, so tea drinkers need not have to worry about lugging along a supply of tea, though.

Drinking chocolate is also available in the supermarkets. There is also even a place called just that, Chocolate, in Sofia, offering delicious chocolate drinks and desserts.

IMPORTED FOOD ITEMS

If you tire of Bulgarian food, there is a wide range of imported goods in the supermarkets. Heinz baked beans, peanut butter, Italian pasta and sauces, real mozarella made from buffalo´s milk, all types of cheeses from different European countries and much more.

There is a shop in Sofia which specialises in cheese called Don des Dieux (Gift of God) at 17 Cherni Vrah Boulevard (across the road from Hilton Hotel) and at 102 Bulgaria Boulevard, business centre `Bellisimo´ .

THE VARIOUS STAGES OF A MEAL

The stages of a meal are typically Western—starters, main course and desserts.

Starters

Starters are usually salads, often taken with *rakia*, and plenty of time. This stage of the meal can take longer than what most Westerners are used to, sometimes up to an hour.

Bulgarian cusine has a wide variety of salads to offer, but *shopska salata* is the Bulgarian pride. It is made with diced tomatoes, cucumbers and peppers and topped with the famous Bulgarian snowy white cheese. When grated egg, mushrooms and sometimes ham are added to *shopska*, it becomes *ovcharska salata* (Shepherd's Salad). The other popular salads are *snezhanka*, which is chopped cucumbers (or gherkins), walnuts and garlic in a creamy yoghurt, *kyopulu*, which is aubergine and bell peppers mashed together with garlic and parsley and *rushka*, a salad made from potatoes, carrots and gherkins with a heavier sauce, mayonnaise.

Other than the mayonnaise of the *rushka*, oil and vinegar are the usual dressing for salads; these duo are always present on restaurant tables.

Hot starters may come after salad, and some are such substantial offerings that non-meat eaters take a selection of these as their main course. Non-meat starters include *bob chorba* (bean soup), *leshta supa* (lentil soup), *tarator* (cold yoghurt and cucumber soup, a sort of diluted version of *Snezhanka*), *chushki burek* (fried peppers stuffed with egg and cheese), *mish mash* (scrambled eggs with chopped tomatoes and peppers), *sirene po shopski* (white cheese, egg and tomatoes baked in a clay

Stomach troubles?

Happily, the rule `cook it, peel it or leave it´ doesn't apply in Bulgaria. Foreigners have eaten salads without trouble. But should you encounter the runs, bananas, rice water or black tea will help. Ginger and garlic are also recommended. Drink lots of water to prevent dehydration. If the opposite problem strikes, eating prunes (available in most supermarkets) really gets the bowel traffic moving again.

pot) and *kashkaval /sirene pane* (fried cheese). Other starters with meat are the Bulgarian favourites, *shkembe chorba,* (tripe soup) and braised chicken hearts or liver.

Two Bulgarian favourites: *kavarma* (top) is a goulash-like spicy meat stew while *tarator* (below) is a cold yoghurt and cucumber soup.

Main Course

A meal isn´t really a meal for Bulgarians without some sort of meat. Meat-free meals are only for the fasting period before Easter and Christmas, or when fasting for economic reasons becomes necessary. Pork, chicken or `veal´ are often grilled, fried or stewed in an earthernware pot. The most common main course dishes are *kyufteta* (spicy meat balls), *kebapcheta* (like *kyufteta*, except moulded into a sausage shape), *kavarma* (a hungarian goulash-like spicy meat stew), *purzhola/kotlet* (chops), *moussaka* (baked layers of mincement and potatoes, similar to the Greek moussaka) and *sarmi* (vine leaves or cabbage stuffed with rice or mincemeat). Chicken or pork chops are often served with fried potatoes and a handful of boiled vegetables, without any sauce.

Desserts

Desserts are the least interesting stage of a Bulgarian culinary experience, unless you like the sweet, sticky desserts common in Turkey and the Middle East, like *baklava* (the nut and filo pastry dessert drowned in syrup), or the more European style cakes with fruits and diet-busting applications of cream. *Garash torta* (a layered chocolate cake) is ubiquitous, as are *sladoled* (ic cream) and *palachinka* (pan cakes).

The better option is Bulgaria´s abundant seasonal fruits: cherries, blueberries, strawberries, raspberries, apples, peaches, plums, watermelons, apricots, grapes and quinces.

RESTAURANTS

Apart from restaurants serving traditional Bulgarian fare, restaurants with international cuisine have multiplied in the main cities, especially in Sofia, in the past few years. If you want a change from Bulgarian, there is Armenian, Italian, French, Serbian, Moroccan, Indian, Japanese and Chinese restaurants or restaurants with a selection of mainstream European food, if you can´t quite decide on which nation´s cuisine until you see the menu.

Posh establishments have sprung up, but service may sometimes slip up. The many difficult years that

Bulgaria has been through has resulted in the country not having enough cordon bleu chefs, sommeliers and trained waiting staff to go round. Five-star hotels and restaurants train their staff from scratch, with problems of poaching by competitors being rampant. That said, the nouveaux riches and the initiated are paving the way to a refinement of tastes.

If the art of fine-dining is still being honed, then the average bistro-type outfits can be a real hit and miss. The food and service vary from very good to waiters simply banging your plates of insipid meal in front of you. The who and what to serve first etiquette is mostly absent. You may be confounded by a waiter asking you how many slices of bread you want, although I find it very practical in not wasting food. When you order mineral water, the wait staff may ask you, "Cold or warm?". Again, I find the question valid, as not everyone likes chilled water. Your dining companion´s food may come long before yours does, so it might be a good idea to forget the common courtesy of waiting for everyone´s food to arrive before eating. To while away the time and forget your gnawing hunger as your companions start with their food, you can read the English menu. Often you will find entertaining gems of translations like `Gordon bleu´, `paper steak´, `charming goose liver´, `fumigated cheese´ and `sub-products´. But just as you prep yourself up for quirky service, especially outside of the cities, they´ll surprise you with friendly and top class service. In a hotel tucked away in Starazagorski Bani (the mineral bath area near Stara Zagora), I was pleasantly surprised by the friendly and efficient restaurant service.

Two things that are almost always served with your food in the average restaurant are cigarette smoke that makes you feel like smoked ham and eardrum-busting music. Although legislation has been introduced for restaurants to have non-smoking areas, they are blatantly ignored. If there is a non-smoking area at all, it´s usually a symbolic pokey corner table surrounded by puffing human chimneys. The music makes conversation impossible.

Two eateries in Sofia that have been cited often as smoke-free and with genuinely background music are the brunch place at the Hilton Sofia and Kibea health food restaurant. The latter is also the place to go, for vegans, vegetarians and people who eat healthy.

Your main course may not always come with accompanying vegetables and/or French fries, and you may have to order them separately. You will also notice that food tends to be served lukewarm, rather than piping hot.

Tipping in restaurants is about 10 per cent. Service charge is sometimes already included in the bill; in this case, you can simply round up the bill. If the wait-staff has been exceptionally good, there´s no harm in rewarding him/her directly, even if service charge is included. Don´t leave the tip on the table when you leave; it´s more polite to hand the tip together with the bill to the wait-staff.

Tipping Tips

- Restaurants, cafes, bars, delivery orders—10 to 15 per cent. If service charge is already included, you can simply round up the bill.
- Taxi drivers expect you to round up the fare. A tip of 10 to 15 per cent (more if the fare is very minimal) is appreciated.
- Petrol stations—a lev or two will be appreciated by the staff who fills your tank and/or cleans your windows
- Barbers, hairdressers—a 10 per cent tip is appreciated
- Hotel chambermaids—a token tip (1 lev to 2 leva for each day of stay) at the end of your stay is appreciated. If there´s a box at the reception desk, you can drop the tip there. If you stay for a long period, drop a tip every fourth day or so. Chances are you´ll get better service therafter.

DO NOT TIP if the service has been wanting. You are not under any obligation to reward poor service.

Outside of Sofia or the main cities, a good meal can be had in a *mehana* (the Bulgarian tavern), offering traditional food.

SNACK SHOPS AND STREET VENDORS

If you´re feeling peckish, you can do what the Bulgarians do; head for any one of the snack shops or street vendors.

The most common snack is the *banitsa* (a piece of flaky pastry filled with cheese, or sometimes meat or spinach). Other popular snacks are pizzas, sandwiches (usually cheese or ham), *ponichki* (deep-fried lumps of dough) and all sorts of nuts sold in paper cones. Sunflower seeds are a hot favourite with the locals; you very often see them expertly getting at the edible kernel and spitting out the shell as they sit in the park or walk along the streets.

There are also plenty of little pastry shops selling the Turkish inspired sweets or European style cakes, as well as shops selling boxes of biscuits (jam-filled, covered with frosted sugar or chocolate etc) prettily displayed in a glass case.

From autumn to spring, there are vendors everywhere selling corn on the cob.

If all these don´t appeal to you, there´s always the good old McDonald´s, Kentucky Fried Chicken, Pizza Hut and Dunkin´ Donuts to fall back on.

DINING ETIQUETTE

Dining etiquette is essentially Western style, with a few Bulgarian traditions to observe.

Bulgarians toast by saying `Nazdrave!´ (meaning health), and look each other in the eyes

What to Say

Nazdrave is Bulgarian for cheers when you propose a toast. It is also what you say when someone sneezes. *Dober Apetit* is the appropriate comment before tucking into a meal.

when doing so. Don´t be surprised if the Bulgarians toast each and every one on the table, unless it´s a rather formal dinner which makes doing so impractical.

Respect is accorded to older people, so even if you are the guest of honour, you should always insist that the eldest person at the table gets the first helping. With Bulgarians, you should forget about your diet for the meal with them. Especially when invited to a Bulgarian´s home, you should eat heartily and try everything. Make sure you have a second helping, to show you like the food. The *rakia* and wine will flow continuously, so if you think you´re not ready to have your glass refilled again, leave a mouthful in your glass. Empty glasses will be filled up automatically.

Note that Bulgarians linger over the salad and starter phase of the meal, so don´t think that that´s the main course itself, especially when you are offered a wide selection of cold cuts and rather substantial starters after a salad.

At formal functions, the ladies may remain seated when newly arrived guests enter the room. The old tradition of a woman not having to stand up when being introduced to a man is still held dear in Bulgaria, even if the man is a minister.

If you need to make small talk, safe topics for conversation are football, Bulgarian cuisine, wine and festivals and their beautiful countryside.

CULTURE AND LEISURE PURSUITS

CHAPTER 7

'A love for tradition has never weakened a nation,
indeed it has strengthened nations in their hour of peril'.
—Winston Churchill

As a country with a varied landscape, Bulgaria offers opportunities to be with unspoilt nature. As descendants of Thracians, Slavs and Bulgars, Bulgarian traditions are a pot-pourri of these cultures, with touches of influences of its neighbours and occupiers. This combination leaves present-day Bulgaria with a rich picking of outdoor activities, fascinating corners to explore and festivals (many steeped in tradition) to experience.

CULTURE
Folk Music
Music is part and parcel of Bulgarian daily life. There are songs for celebrations, to accompany arduous work, or to express sorrow. There are songs for Christmas, for harvesting, when praying for rain, melancholic songs of the *gourbetchii* (seasonal migrant workers) pining for home and family far away, and songs to mark rites of passage like weddings and leaving home for military service. Bulgarian folk music is sometimes described as homophonic; the song sounds single-voiced even if a number of people are singing. Some villages have developed a polyphonic style, with women singing in two- or three-part harmony, with occasional whoops and vibrati. Bulgarian music is unique for its rhythmic complexities.

Musical Instruments
The traditional instruments are the *gaida*, the *kaval*, the *gadulka*, the *tambura* and the *tupan*. The *gaida* is a bagpipe

Making music with the gaida in the park.

A group of folk musicians play modern musical instruments in the style true to traditional instruments.

made from goat skin. The *gaida* from the Rhodope Mountain region, caled *kaba gaida*, is bigger and has a deeper sound. The *kaval*, an end-blown flute, is a shepherd´s instrument, like the gaida. The *gadulka* and the *tambura* are stringed instruments; the *gadulka* is held vertically when played. The *tupan* is a large drum played on one side with a drum-stick and a thinner stick on the other.

More recently, the clarinet, saxophone, accordion, bass and violin have become popular instruments, but are played in a style true to traditional instruments.

Chalga

Traditonalists may scoff at *chalga*, but no mention of Bulgarian music can fail to mention this modern-day phenomenon called *chalga*. Started in the early 1990s, *chalga* music is in-your-face pop-folk, often featuring peroxide blondes writhing in very little clothes. The most famous is Azis, an androgynous person who looks like George Michael when in a conservative mood and Boy George, when feeling flamboyant, complete with mini-skirt. *Chalga* is not just music; like rap, it´s a sub-culture. Basically a reaction to the tight lid placed on foreign ´decadent´ music during the communist era, *chalga* is all about making money fast and lauding mini skirts. Love it or hate it, *chalga* is so popular that many of the political parties had *chalga* singers as crowd-pullers on their campaign trail for the European parliament elections in 2007.

If you´re curious, ask a Bulgarian friend to take you to a *chalga* disco, and don´t forget to get them to translate the lyrics for you.

Dance

Bulgarian folk dances are usually line dances and the movement is dignified. There are some dance routines which are energetic, with fancy footwork, and with shorter lines comprising a few dancers, and they move around in a rather adrenalin-pumping pace. For a layman like me, I would say that the dances resemble Greek folk dances, or even the Cossack dances, especially for the more energetic executions. The dances vary differently, naturally, from region to region.

Folk Costume

The first thing that hits you about the folk costume is the rich colours. You will then marvel at the intricate embroidery, including on the men´s shirts and jackets. Other typical features in women´s costumes are the aprons, sometimes worn over pinafore-like garments, and the intricate belt buckles. Head-gear is also common for both men and women, and for the latter, they range from simple scarves to elaborate decorations of flowers, silver decorations and pom poms. Like the dances, the costumes can be broadly said to be similar to the Greek and Cossack costumes.

Experiencing Folk Culture

To get an idea of what traditional folk music and dance is like, flick through the local TV channels and you are sure to come across some performance or other. Some restaurants, like the Chevermeto in Sofia, also have live performances for their guests.

Anyone interested in having a more in-depth knowledge of Bulgarian folk music and dance can attend the Bulgarian Folk Music and Dance Seminar, which takes place from around 29 July to 5 August. The programme is designed for non-Bulgarians desiring a more in-depth learning opportunity. Organised by the Academy of Music, Dance & fine Arts in Plovdiv, the seminar is conducted by professional teachers. The seminar is held during this time to specially coincide with the Bulgarian Folk Festivals taking place in the region, so that participants can observe the performances first-hand.

More details can be found at http://www.folkseminarplovdiv. com/index.cfm

Opera

With singing second-nature to Bulgarians, it´s not surprising that the country has churned out many world-class opera singers. Opera aficionados might wrack their brains, though, to think of even one famous Bulgarian opera singer. Bulgaria fell off most people´s radar screen after 500 years under the Ottoman Empire and thereafter subdued by the Soviet Union. Furthermore, most of them spent their professional life outside of Bulgaria, leaving people to associate them with their country of residence or assume that they were Russians, given their Slavic names. Boris Christoff, Ghena Dimitrova, Vesselina Kasanova and Rayna Kabaivanska are examples of top Bulgarian operatic talent.

Church Music

A Bulgarian church service is made so much more magical not only by the beautiful icons in church, but also by the religious chanting. Fans of Gregorian chants will surely find Bulgarian chants enchanting.

Handicrafts

Bulgarians have a strong tradition in pottery, embroidery, weaving, woodwork, copperwork and silverwork. Although such skills were developed to produce items for everyday use, many of the traditional crafts are souvenir items today, such as the lace from Kalofer, silver filigree brooches and pendants, kilims and carpets, ceramic pots and bowls, wooden jewellery boxes and hand-painted icons.

PUBLIC HOLIDAYS

1-2 January	New Year's Holiday
3 March	Liberation Day (Treaty of San Stefano in 1878)
April	Easter*
1 May	Labour Day
6 May	Gergyovden (St. George's Day), and Bulgarian Army Day
24 May	Bulgarian Education and Culture, and Slavonic Literature Day
6 September	Unification Day (unification of the Principality of Bulgaria with Eastern Rumelia in 1885)
22 September	Independence Day (declaration of independence from Ottoman rule)
25 December	Christmas Day

* date varies as it follows the Julian calendar

FESTIVALS

In a lot of ways, Bulgaria is like a live cultural show. If you happen to be in a rural village at the right time, you can still catch the villagers in folk costume celebrating some ancient festival the same way it was done by their forefathers, complete with the traditional music and dance mentioned

Bulgarians are proud of their traditions and a group of strangers perform an impromptu *horo* folk dance while in a park.

above. An English lady remarked to me sotto voce as we watched a folk dance being performed that no young man in her country would be seen dead dressed in folk costume and performing a traditional dance nowadays. That is the case with the younger generation in many countries. The Bulgarians, however, are so proud of their traditions that people of all ages would join in a *horo* dance at the drop of a *kalpak* (traditonal Bulgarian hat), including city folks. Folk dance groups are not comprised of senior citizens; they include young men and women. There is a historical, psychological background to why traditions have been upheld so tenaciously: keeping Bulgarian traditions was a way to show that they would not be overcome or subdued by their occupiers, especially during the five hundred years under the Ottoman Turks.

Most Bulgarian festivals are born of a mix of religious and pagan traditions. During the communist era, although religious practices were not officially banned, it was ridiculed by the communists. Agents of the communist party lurked in churches and reported anyone caught going to church to the party officials. Although religious practices were condemned, practices that were pagan in nature were allowed. In some cases, the religious roots of certain practices were substituted with a neutral or nationalist background—Father Christmas became Grandpa Frost, and the red colour of easter eggs became representative of the blood of Bulgarian soldiers, instead of the blood of Christ. With the fall of communism, religious practices were resurrected with fervour, by the devout who were happy to be able to practise their religion openly once again and by the anti-communists to make a clear cut with the communist past.

Some festivals are confined to a particular region, while others are celebrated all over the country. There is an inexhaustible list of festivals that are celebrated by the Bulgarians, so those listed below are just a selection of the more popular or intriguing ones. Many of the guide books (e.g. *Insider's Guide* and *Rough Guide*) have compiled detailed lists of the festivals which make fascinating reading, for readers who are into festivals and other cultural activities.

Spring
Baba Marta (1 March)
On the first day of March, Bulgarians wish each other *Chestita Baba Marta* (Happy Grandmother Marta). The tradition dates back to time immemorial and welcomes spring (personified by a temperamental grandmother with a name, Marta, derived from the Bulgarian word for March). Bulgarians give each other a *martenitsa* (plural *martenitsi*), a red and white tassle made from wool, to bring the recipient health, prosperity and good luck. Depending on who you ask, the white symbolises the snow in winter, and the red, the sun returning in spring, or that the white represents the fair complexion of a lady and the red, her rosy cheeks. Traditional *martenitisi* are either a red and white plait or a pair of male and female woollen dolls (called Pizho and Penda respectively) but the designs are becoming more creative each year. The *martenitsa* is worn on the wrist or like a brooch, until the wearer spots the first stork (a sign that spring has arrived), whereupon it is hung on a tree or left under a slab of stone. If left under a stone, the owner returns nine days later to find what is underneath the stone; ants would promise a prosperous year, while spiders would be a bad omen. Others throw their *martenitsi* into rivers, so

that their lives will flow smoothly like the river. The practice varies from region to region. Spotting storks is a bit tricky for city dwellers, so nowadays the wearer can remove the *martenitsa* when he/she sees the first green shoot.

In the last weeks of February, the streets start filling up with stalls selling *martenitsi*, lending a festive cheer to the otherwise chilly temperatures. There is a carnival atmosphere, as people of all ages throng the stalls, choosing from the different designs. It reminded me of shopping in Chinatown.

Throughout March, one often catches sight of Bulgarians walking around with a *martenitsa* tied to their wrist or worn brooch-style. Even the pet pooches are not forgotten. Most of the four-legged members of the family have a *martenitsa* on their collar as well.

By the end of March, most shrubs in the parks are festooned with *martenitsi*.

A selection of traditional *martenitisi* which are made of red and white wool.

International Women´s Day (8 March)

This day is celebrated in Bulgaria like a combination of Mother´s Day and Valentine´s Day. On the streets , you will see happy women of all ages clutching a stalk or a bunch of flowers. Some men also have flowers in their hands, as they hurry to bring the flowers to the intended recipient. Although it falls on the same day as the UN sponsored International Women´s Day, the celebrations in Bulgaria has communist roots, when this day honoured the `Heroic Women Worker´, and just for this one day, women were treated with special courtesy. Some Bulgarian women see this date as discriminatory, though, and ignore it.

Thrace Day (26 March)

Since 2006, 26 March is an official holiday, after intensive lobbying by the Union of Thracian Societies. On 26 March 1913, Bulgarian troops managed to pry the Edirne fortress from Ottoman fingers, and as you would realise by now, anything that is a triumph over the Ottomans is a source of pride and joy. The event is commemorated with solemn parades and patriotic speeches. The Bulgarians proudly identify themselves as descendants of Thracians and see the

Waiting patiently for the start of speeches to mark Thrace Day on 26 March.

area which was once Thrace as rightfully Bulgarian. That parts of it today lie in northern Greece and Turkey is a constant source of irritation.

Easter (varies, as it follows the Julian calendar)

Easter (*Velikden*, meaning Great Day) in Bulgaria (which follows the Julian calendar) does not always fall on the same day as Easter according to the Gregorian calendar used by the Western church, but in some years (like 2004 and 2007), they do.

On the Sunday six weeks before Easter, devout Christians start fasting, which means abstaining from everything that is derived from animals, including eggs and dairy products.

The Saturday before Palm Sunday is a significant day especially for Bulgarian village communities. Lazarovden is a day for coming-out celebrations of sorts. The young girls would gather in one of the young lady's home and from there, go round the village singing songs praising the maiden's beauty, the industry of the farmer and wishes for happiness and prosperity.

Palm Sunday (*Tsvetnitsa-Vrabnitsa*) is one of the biggest Bulgarian holidays, marking Jesus' entry into Jerusalem, as well as being a Name Day for everyone named after flowers or plants. Bulgarian Orthodox tradition uses the more readily available willow branches instead of palm, and on Palm Sunday, the branches are blessed in church before being hung up at home for health and luck. Male and female youngsters also wear crowns made from willow. Although still during the fasting period, fish is allowed on Palm Sunday.

Like many Western traditions, eggs are also an important feature in Bulgarian Easter as it similarly symbolises new life and resurrection. The week before Easter, eggs are sold in trays of 30's, instead of the usual half dozen or dozen boxes. Eggs are dyed on Maundy Thursday or Saturday. When the mother dyes the eggs, the first one must be dyed in red (symbolising the blood of Christ) and is used to draw a cross on the forehead of her children to bring them health. This first Egg is then kept until the next year's Easter. On

The Orthodox church uses willow branches as a blessing on Palm Sunday.

no account should eggs be dyed on Good Friday. Easter eggs are not hidden around the house for the egg-hunt as is done in Western tradition, but take centre stage on the table and will be used for the 'egg challenge' (explained further down).

Kozunak (or *Kolache*) at Easter is to Bulgarians what hot cross buns are to the British on Good Friday. It's a sweet-tasting bread, mostly round in shape, although some are more elongated. In recent years, Italian *panetonne* is starting to replace the traditional version.

On the Saturday before Easter, Bulgarians go to church for the special service just before midnight, bringing the eggs with them for blessing. At midnight, the priest emerges with a lighted candle, with which the congregation will light their own candles before they all walk round the church

Kozunak are a special bread that is baked at Easter in Bulgaria.

three times. The candle is to be brought home and whoever manages to bring their candle safely home without its getting snuffed out will have untold luck. The eggs are used for tapping against someone else's egg. The traditional greeting is *Christos Voskrese* (Christ has risen) and the response of the congregation is *Voistina Voskrese* (indeed He has risen).

Easter Sunday lunch involves a table groaning with food, especially the all important lamb. For married couples, there is a tradition to have lunch with the family of one's best man. Before tucking in, however, the great egg challenge takes place. Everyone knocks their easter eggs against each other's, and the person's with the egg which remains uncracked to the last is the winner. The egg challenge is a popular tradition and I've seen young couples meeting up in the park on Easter Monday with coloured eggs for this ritual before comsuming the eggs.

Commercialism has started creeping into Easter celebrations. Chocolate eggs and decorative items in the shape of chicks and coloured eggs are sold in supermarkets and stalls in the streets.

Slavonic Literacy and Culture Day (24 May)

This day essentially honours the revered St. Cyril and Methodius, founders of the Cyrillic alphabet. Students weave greenery, branches and flowers into garlands to be placed above their school entrances and to frame pictures of the two saints. Apart from church services, there are dance performances and choral groups made up of students and their teachers in public areas. Of course the Cyril and Methodius anthem is sung.

Summer

Rose Festival in the Valley of the Roses (First weekend of June)

Rose festivals take place in Kazanluk and Karlovo, with folk music and parades. Don´t expect to see beautiful local lasses picking roses, though; roses are harvested in May in the early hours of the morning, when you´d prefer to be still tucked up in bed.

Folklore festivals

From June through August, folklore festivals take place in various regions in the country. There's fire-dancing at Bulgari village in the Strandzha mountains on or about 4 June. Indians might be surprised that fire-walking is done in Bulgaria, but it´s a tradition in some villages in the Strandzha mountains. Fire dancers walk on hot coals to mark St. Constantine and Helen Day. This ritual was anathema to the Orthodox church and banned by the communists, but survived in secret and is making a comeback. Not intended to be a tourist attraction, the ritual nonetheless draws fascinated foreigners. It´s best not to try it yourself, though, as it is believed only people who have been `called´ are able to dance on the coals without landing up in hospital.

Autumn

Yet more folklore festivals take place, as well as a wine harvest festival in Melnik, and an International Jazz Forum each in Ruse (end October), in Blagoevgrad (November) and in Sofia (also November).

Winter

St. Nicholas Day/Nikulden (6 December)

On this day, Bulgarians celebrate the day of the patron saint of the sea, rivers, lakes, fishermen and sailors. He is also revered as the guardian of the family.

Fish, especially *ribnik* (stuffed carp) is a must in every home, a special exception from the pre-Christmas fasting period. As with all festivals, ritual bread must also be baked. Tradition dictates that the bones of the carp should be burned, buried in the ground or dropped in the river, to bring the family fertility and well-being.

This date is also the Name Day for those named Nikola, Nikolay, Nikolin, Nina, Neno and Nenka.

Christmas Day/Koleda (25 December)

Although Easter follows the Julian calendar, Christmas is calculated according to the Gregorian calendar, so it falls on 25 December instead of 6 January. Devout Christians start fasting 40 days before Christmas, abstaining from all food derived from animals, including milk and yoghurt. The fasting is to purify the body and soul before Christmas.

Christmas is celebrated among family members and very close friends or neighbours. On Christmas eve, a lot of rituals are followed to ensure that the following year would be a good one. Old traditions dictated that a Yule log (*Budnik*), from an oak or pear tree, is kept burning all throughout the night. Another important feature is the ritual bread, or rather, the three different types of bread, one dedicated to Christmas, one to the house and farm and the third to be given to the *koledari* (the carol singers). Nowadays, although old traditions may be harder to keep for the city dwellers, many still observe whatever old traditions they can, such as having nine, eleven or thirteen different meatless dishes and the ritual bread. Typical dishes are stuffed peppers, beans, *banitsa*, stuffed vine leaves, pickles, walnuts, apples and *ushaf* (boiled dried fruits). The tradition is to eat sitting on the floor. A silver coin and special messages (health, success, love, a new car etc) are baked into the ritual bread, and at the start of the meal, the oldest man will break the ritual bread into pieces, with

Street vendors selling Christmas ornaments in Sofia.

the first piece dedicated to the family´s welfare and health, and the rest distributed to everyone around the table, starting with the older males. The person who gets the piece with the silver coin will have untold luck. The rest have to console themselves with seeing which fortune message they get, not unlike fortune cookies. No one should leave the table during the meal, and the table is not cleared after the meal, but left for the deceased who will return to feast.

At midnight in the villages, the *koledari* dressed in folk costume will go round the neighbourhood singing. They are normally given a special ring-shaped bun as well as other food and money. In Sofia, the only *koledari* you will see are probably at special Christmas concerts.

On 25 December itself, fasting is over and Bulgarians go back to meat dishes.

New Year's Day (1 January)

New Year celebrations is less confined to the family and more party time. In Sofia, a free open-air concert takes place in front of the National Art Gallery (the former Tsar's palace) and shortly before midnight, the President's speech is broadcast to the nation. Then the crowd counts down and at midnight, they play the national anthem and everyone sings. Dancing the *horo* (the circular dance with everyone linking hands) follows, with fireworks lighting up the sky.

Wherever you are in Bulgaria, you will find people dancing the horo just after midnight. Young children go around with a twig from the cornel tree, called *sourvaknitsa*, tapping members of the family on the back to bring them good luck and health. In the cities, if you're out in the streets, you may be tapped by young children in the hope of some cash in return.

New Year's Day in 2007 will always be a special one in the history of Bulgaria. The country became an EU member state on this day, and one second into 1 January 2007, special celebrations took place all over the country, tempered only by a hint of sadness over the Bulgarian medics still imprisoned in Libya then. While a special light and fireworks show went on in Battenberg Square in Sofia, Bulgarians elsewhere celebrated their EU membership in traditional style by spit-roasting a 600 kg ox.

Yordanovden (6 January)

If you happen to be near a body of water on this day, and suddenly see topless men hovering on the edge of the lake or sea, it's not that they have had too much *rakiya*. These men are getting ready to rush into the water to retrieve a cross thrown by an Orthodox priest. The person who gets to the cross first will be lucky and healthy for the whole year.

This day is commemorated by the Orthodox church as the day of Jesus' baptism in the River Jordan, hence the connection with water. It's also the name day of those called Yordan/ka, Daniel/a, Bozhan/a, Bogomil/a, and these Yordans, Bozhans and Daniels are expected to take a plunge into the icy waters.

Kukeri Processions in Pernik (23 January)

Kukeri processions take place in other parts of the country on different dates in late winter or early spring, but this tradition is similar everywhere. The Kukeri ritual is intended to scare away evil spirits and bring fertility. Only males take part in the ritual, wearing terrifying masks made with fur, feathers and horns and noisy bells around their waists.

Sahara Creeps Over Bulgarian Fields and Orchards

An unprecedented drought ruins wheat, roses and peach orchards in Bulgaria. Cracks the size of a fist have opened in the fields in Dobrudja, considered Bulgaria's granary. The land is desert dry and wheat has withered. If Heaven has no mercy on us, our land will soon turn into a Sahara. Bulgaria's granary is dying, farmers from Dobrudja complain. It has not been that dry for thirty-three years when the wheat crop was half the normal and now all points that this year is going to be even worse

People from all corners of Bulgaria are getting ready to hold church services and perform old pagan rituals to lure in the rain.

Tomorrow, girls from the village of Chelopek, near Vratsa (northwestern Bulgaria) will put on elder-twig skirts for the *Peperuda* (Butterfly) rite. The youngest, who is the embodiment of a butterfly, will wear a shirt only and be barefooted. The other girls accompany the "butterfly" touring the village spinning and chanting: "The butterfly whirls and the butterfly prays, please Lord, let it rain to fill barns with grain". Every housewife pours water through a sieve over the butterfly girl. Older women remember that the rain cloud appear even before the whole ritual was over. Rarely, though, it happens that the Butterfly fails to bring rain and then grannies usually take the matter in their hands.

They take out a clay male figurine with a huge phallus decorated with wheat and rye grains. They carry it around water fountains and wells and finally bury the figurine near the river. This pagan ritual is called Gherman and is forbidden for maidens but has never failed to bring the rain and good harvest. ´

—Standart News 16 May 2007 (http://www.standartnews.com)

Author´s Note: Astoundingly, two days later, heavy downpours came down on Bulgaria and continued for more than a week..

Valentine´s and St. Trifon Zarezan Day (14 February)

This date has traditionally been an important day in Bulgaria, not because it´s Valentine´s Day, but because this day honours St. Trifon Zarezan, the patron saint of wine.

St. Trifon Zarezan´s Day is so popular that the Bulgarians celebrate it on both 14 February and 1 February, that is, the day calculated according to the Gregorian and the Julian calendars. The key ritual on this day is the pruning of the vines, something which only the men are allowed to do. The women´s duty is to bake the ritual bread, stuff and roast the chicken, and put these into a woolen bag with a flask of wine for their menfolk to take to the performance of the ritual. The ritual involves pruning three vines and pouring red wine over the cut places. Once the pruning is done, the men gather to drink and make merry together.

In recent years, St.Valentine has come to compete for attention with St. Trifon. Since the fall of communism in 1989, Valentine´s Day has steadily gained commercial success. Nowadays, as in many other countries, the shops are full of Valentine cards, chocolates and heart-shaped everything.

LEISURE PURSUITS
Expatriates always complain that there isn´t very much to do on weekends here. This is true if you´re looking to replicate the way you spend your weekends at home. But if you keep an open mind, and admit that on some weekends back home, you did feel bored out of your skull with doing the same thing again, it isn´t so bad as congenital grumblers make it out to be in Bulgaria. For lovers of nature, there is in fact so much to explore that many expatriates never manage to go to all the interesting places during their time in the country. Whether you´re into sports, history, geology, archeology, folk culture, nature or just a beach bum, you will be able to pursue your interests substantially in Bulgaria.

Classical Music
Classsical music buffs can enjoy operas and performances by various orchestras in Sofia. Sofia´s National Opera can seat 1,200 and perform familiar favourites from Mozart, Puccini and the like. Bulgaria Hall is the venue to catch the Sofia Philharmonic Orchestra, Sofia Chamber Orchestra,

New Symphony Orchestra (a private orchestra), choirs, performances by young virtuosi from the National Music Academy and other classical music performances.

Prices for performances are a very reasonable. *The Sofia Echo* provides an extremely helpful listing of what´s on in the various venues each week. The newspaper also provides information on the events held in the various cultural institutes (French, German, Czech, Polish etc).

In major cities like Plovdiv, Varna and Ruse, you can also expect to find opera houses, concert halls and a host of classical programmes.

Galleries and Museums

The National Art Gallery (in the former Tsar´s Palace) traces Bulgarian art from 18th century to modern-day, while the gallery in the crypt of the Alexander Nevski Church focuses on old Bulgarian art, especially icons. Sofia City Art Gallery showcases the mostly 20th century works of Bulgarian artists. Foreign artists´ works are featured in the National Gallery for Foreign Art. There are also many smaller private galleries for art lovers to browse in.

The National History Museum in Boyana, the suburbs of Sofia, is the museum with over 650,000 exhibits starting from pre-historic times, including the Thracian gold and silver treasures. The problem is that most of the most prized items are on tour outside of Bulgaria, as a `humanitarian aid for needy museums in the West´, according to the museum director. While in Boyana, one shouldn´t miss going about 2 km (1.25 miles) away to see the Boyana Church, which is on the UNESCO World Cultural Heritage list. This small church tucked away in a garden among the trees dates back to the 11th century. A guide will accompany you inside, where you can feast your eyes on the frescoes, painted by an unkown artist around 1259. A museum nearby allows visitors to learn more about the history of the church and muse over replicas of the frescoes. In Sofia itself, the National Archeological Museum also has an interesting collection of Thracian, Greek and Roman treasures. Ladies will marvel at how exquisite the jewellery of those times were. Bulgarian folklore and traditions

The Ethnographic Museum in Plovdiv is housed in a magnificient building that dates back to the 19th century.

can be soaked up at the Ethnographic Museum in the east wing of the National Art gallery. If you like oggling at animals in formalin, pop down to the Natural History Museum; for gemstones, check out the Earth and Man Museum.

In Bulgarian museums, you often have to pay an extra 10 leva (80 leva for use of videos in the National History Museum!) if you wish to take photos. If you´re used to European museums where photography is not forbidden, or even encouraged, you will find it rather illogical why Bulgarian museums don´t want you to ´show off´ their exhibits on their behalf.

Art galleries can be found in the other major cities, and practically all cities and towns are never lacking in museums, even if it´s a small one. National pride ensures that there is always at least a house museum to showcase the birthplace of a famous Bulgarian or an ethnographic museum to immortalise local culture. Varna´s Archeological Museum houses an outstanding collection of Thracian and Roman artefacts.

Cinemas

There are a multitude of cinemas and a three-dimensional IMAX cinema in Bulgaria with a 18 m (59 feet) high and 24 m (78 feet) wide screen in Sofia. Cinemas can be found in the Euro-Bulgarian Cultural Centre, the underpass in front of NDK, Sofia City Centre and Mall of Sofia. The IMAX theatre is in the Mall of Sofia. Most films are in its original English or French, with Bulgarian subtitles. Again, the *Sofia Echo* is the authority on what is playing where in Sofia.

---

http://www.programata.bg

This website lets you search for information on classical music, concerts, movies, restaurants, videos and DVDs, club music and more for Sofia, Plovdiv, Varna, Burgas and Stara Zagora.

Casinos

Gaming urges can be satisfied in the many casinos in Bulgarian cities, as well as in the country's resorts. Most of them are located in hotels, though there are private establishments as well. Only licenced casinos are allowed

Catering to your gambling urges is this casino in a market.

to operate gaming equipment. There is even a casino in the market, among stalls selling cheap clothing, but it´s best to exercise caution where you try out your luck. The gambling business in Bulgaria has an annual turnover of more than 600 million Euros.

Monuments/ Noteworthy Buildings
Sofia and Environs
What is so pleasant about Sofia is that the city has a significant number of historical monuments, some very grand, all within walking distance of one another (unless you´re an incorrigible couch potato). Most of them are in the vicinity of a five-star hotel (Hilton, Sheraton, Radisson) which makes it easy for newcomers to direct a taxi there or ask your way around.

In the vicinity of Hilton Hotel
You can´t miss the monstrous building next to the Hilton Hotel, the National Palace of Culture, which the Bulgarians call NDK (pronounced En De Kah) which stands for *Natsionalen Dvorets na Kulturata*. This concrete giant, built to commemorate 1,300 years of Bulgarian statehood today houses concert halls, conference facilities and office space as well a below-ground, unexciting shopping area. In front

The massive NDK building is home to various leisure options and is beside a large park which attracts skateboarders.

of the concrete building is an expansive concrete park, where novice skateboarders and mountain bikers test out their capabilities. The monstrous structure jutting out behind a fence with creative grafitti is the Bulgaria 1300 years monument. There is also a small piece of the Berlin Wall in one corner of the park, to commemorate the unification of East and West Europe. There is also a tiny chapel, seemingly defiant amidst these socialist symbols. At the end of the park (away from NDK), is the start of Bulgaria´s Oxford Street. Vitosha Boulevard is almost a pedestrian mall, save for the tram, bicycles, traffic crossing at right angles to it, and drivers who insist on breaking the law.

In the vicinity of Sheraton Hotel

After oggling at the shops along Vitosha Boulevard, you end up at the Palace of Justice on your left. On your right is the Sheraton Hotel and the Sveta Nedelya Church. This is the historic centre of Sofia. Sveta Nedelya is the infamous church which saw an attempt on the life of Tsar Boris III when the communist terrorists detonated a bomb killing more than 100 people in 1925.

Carrying along straight on Vitosha Boulevard past Sveta Nedelya Church will bring you onto Maria Luisa Boulevard,

The 1300 years monument: A prime example of Sofia's numerous communist era structures of questionable aesthetic taste

The Sveta Nedelya Church is located within Sofia's historic centre.

The interior of St. Georges Rotunda showcases many beautiful frescoes.

where you will come across the Sveta Petka Samadzhiiska church (the roof just barely visible at street level), TZUM shopping centre, the Banya Bashi Mosque and the Central Baths on your right. At No. 4 Budapeshta Street is the new hotel, Arena di Serdica (opened on 25 Jan 2007), which artfully integrates into the building a 3rd century amphitheatre, discovered during construction of the hotel. On your left is the covered market (Halite), Pirotska Street, the only truly vehicle-free street, the Synagogue and slightly farther away, the Zhenski Pazaar.

Behind the Sheraton Hotel is the St. George Rotunda, a 4th century treasure with a red brick exterior. Although modest-looking from the outside, there are some beautiful frescoes inside. Coming out at the other end of the courtyard, you will see the Presidency, with the guard of honour (in very different uniforms in summer and winter) attracting tourists all the time. Opposite the Presidency is the National Archaeological Museum, dating from 1494. This former mosque has nine domes and houses interesting Thracian, Greek and Roman treasures. Just behind the Museum is the City Garden from where you can see the Ivan Vasov Theatre (a beautiful building designed by Austrian architects and built in 1907) and the former Tsar´s palace, now the National Art Gallery. Down the road from the Tsar´s Palace is the supersized Party House, office space of the Communist Central Committee formerly and now, the parliament.

In the vicinity of Radisson Hotel
Standing at the entrance of Radisson, you´ll be able to see in a straight line of vision the Tsar Osvoboditel monument, the National Assembly (parliament house) and the pièce de résistance of Sofia, the Alexander Nevski Cathedral. The cathedral is one of the finest pieces of architecture in the Balkans and is a memorial to the Russian casualties in the war to liberate Bulgaria from the Ottomans. The domes, covered in gold leaf donated by Russia in 1960, glisten spectacularly on a sunny day, and no visitor to Sofia should miss seeing this crown jewel of the city. In the crypt below the cathedral is an excellent collection of icon painting, a few dating back

The Alexander Nevski Cathedral contains a treasure trove of Bulgarian art.

to medieval times. Just behind the cathedral is the Sveta Sofia church, which dates back to late Roman times, although the building has been much rebuilt after being damaged by earthquakes and invaders.

The unique yellow bricks on the road running along the front of the National Assembly were a present from Austrian emperor Franz Josef to his cousin, Prince Ferdinand of Saxe-Coburg. Farther down Tsar Osvoboditel Road is the beautiful Russian Church. To the east of the Radisson Hotel is the seat of learning, Sofia University.

Outside Sofia

Monuments are not restricted to Sofia alone, naturally. The pride and adulation the Bulgarians have for their revolutionary or National Revival heroes like Vasil Levski, Hristo Botev, Paisii of Hilendar and Neofit Rilski, and for their poets and other men of letters guarantee that there is at least a monument in each of their place of birth. Such a monument of Vasil Levski stands in Karlovo, a gigantic statue of Hristo Botev overlooks the main square in Kalofer and in Bansko, a monument remembers Father Paisii (whose *Slav-Bulgarian History* was the catalyst for the National Revival) and a house museum is dedicated to Neofit Rilski (another key figure in Bulgarian education during the Revival).

The old city area of Plovdiv is a living museum of National Revival Period orieled houses standing proudly in cobbled streets. The richly decorated interior of the Hindlian House has tourists spell-bound and the Ethnographic Museum with its beautifully decorated exterior has cameras clicking away all the time. If it´s old European-style architecture you´re after, Ruse is the answer.

Monasteries and Churches

If you share Prince Charles´ fascination with monasteries, you will get more than your fill in Bulgaria.

Rila Monastery, the poster-boy of Bulgarian monasteries, is not only magnificent architecturally, but is also situated in a magical location with the imposing Rila massif in the background. Although the monastery was plundered and then burnt down in 1833, the re-built version is no less awesome. Other famous monasteries include the Bachkovo Monastery (Bulgaria´s second largest) and Troyan Monastery (the third largest), although there are many more. Many monasteries also have somber histories, such as Dryanovski, which was the base for plotting a local uprising against the Ottomans in 1876 and where several hundred rebels were slaughtered. Others are unusual in that they are carved into the rock such as the St. Dimiter Bassarbovski Monastery some 10 km (6.2 miles) south of Ruse.

The frescoes, iconostases, icons and wood carvings in the churches are awe-inspiring. The Alexander Nevski church in Sofia, the Holy Virgin Church of Rila Monastery, the monastery church of Troyan Monastery, the Church of St. Constantine and Helen in Plovdiv, the Church of the Nativity in Arbanasi and the churches of Nessebur are some excellent examples of the beauty of Bulgarian churches. The rock churches of Ivanovo, some 18 km (11 miles) south of Ruse, have lovely medieval frescoes too.

Archaeological and Medieval Sites

Given the long and varied history of this country, it is no small wonder that there are many archaeological sites. Kazanluk´s

Observing Basic Courtesy

If you intend to go into any religious building, make sure you're modestly covered. Backless dresses, too much cleavage and shorts are no-nos. A big scarf or shawl in your bag will come in handy when popping into churches, mosques or synagogues if you're wearing a spaghetti top in summer.

Women should cover their heads when going into a mosque, synagogue or the Russian Orthodox Church. Before taking photos, check for signs to see if it's allowed.

Valley of the Thracian Kings, Stara Zagora's neolithic dwellings and Roman theatre, Nessebur's Architectural, Historical and Archaeological Reserve and the Tsarevets Fortress of Veliko Turnovo are but just a few.

Geographical Wonders

Bulgaria has some fascinating rock formations, some of which are similar to the famed tufa formations in Cappadocia, Turkey. The Kurdzhali region in the Eastern Rhodopes, the village of Stob (about 5 km/3.1 miles southwest of Rila), showcase what is often called pyramids (although they look more like a group of tall stalagmites rather than the Giza Pyramid). Arguably the most spectacular is the 90 sq.km (34.7 sq.miles) of limestone pinnacles in Belogradchik. The gorges (such as the spectacular Trigrad Gorge complete with waterfall and the famous cave Devil's Throat which swallows up the River Trigradska), lakes, caves, changing vegetation as you ascend the Rila Mountains (oaks, elms, ashes, to beeches, birches, aspens to white fir and black fir and then finally Alpine grass at the top) will ensure that geography class is never going to be boring again.

Spas

Situated at the foot of Mt. Vitosha is the Dream Spa & Fitness, a pampering paradise with hydro-massaging pools, whirlpools, Finnish sauna, solariums, cafe and nursery. Victoria Spa (specialising in Asian spa treatments) recently opened a spa in Ambassador Hotel in Sofia.

Bulgaria has many springs offering all sorts of health solutions, but its spa potential has not been maximised, but steps are underway to develop spa tourism. Kustendil, Velingrad, Bansko, Katarino and Hisarya are some of Bulgaria's most well known spa destinations.

The Parks

If you wish to stroll amidst nature, read a book or your child or dog is crying for a `walkie-walkie´, you are spoiled for choice with the numerous parks in Sofia. The oldest is the City Garden, with the Ivan Vazov theatre, alfresco cafes, fountains and an Art Nouveau newspaper kiosk lending it an air of `Old Europe´. The biggest is Boris´ Garden, designed by a Swiss in 1880. Although slightly jaded now, the park still impresses with its sheer size and some charming areas, like around the fountain. In the sprawling grounds are tennis courts, a go-cart track, playgrounds, cafes, children´s bicycles and cars for rental, and an adventure playground for the kids behind Park Hotel Moskva. Yuzhen Park is slightly more socialist in taste, with a lot of fairground attractions on weekends like trampolines, all sorts of rides, simple cafes and popcorn, candy floss and nut vendors. The playgrounds are distinctly more run down than those in Boris´ Garden, but nonetheless very utilised on weekends. Doctor´s Garden is a small, but well-kept area, no small thanks to the `Friends of Doctors´ Garden´, a group of volunteers who lovingly look after it. This garden boasts a small collection of archeological remains from Roman times. Near the Sofia University, in front of the National Library and also the NDK are open

Enjoying a ride in the children's playground.

Yuzhen Park offers various activities and a good view of Mt. Vitosha.

areas with benches where one can sit and people-watch or read, although it´s a little bit too heavy on the concrete side for lovers of greenery.

Some 3 km (1.86 miles) southeast of Yuzhen Park is the Zoopark, a concrete, sun-baked zoo with tigers, leopards and bears, and some cafes. Another open area for the young ones to enjoy is Pantilantsi, an indoor and outdoor amusement area in the district of Mladost III.

In practically all cities, there will be a public park with cared-for flower beds (or so it seems to me). Coastal town like Varna and Burgas have what are called Maritime Gardens; huge parks next to the sea.

Nature parks also abound in Bulgaria. The advantage of living in Sofia is that a half hour´s drive will bring you out to the Vitosha Nature Park, with different trails for you to choose on a whim. Other nature parks are spread all over the country, essentially to protect the flora and fauna of the area, with Rila National Park being the biggest of Bulgaria´s national parks.

Birdwatching

The Bill Oddie or John James Audubon among us will take delight in the abundant opportunities for birding in Bulgaria. The forests, lakes and marshes will satisfy even the most serious twitcher with the roll-call of landbirds, waders, waterfowls, raptors etc. Just walking in the parks will bring you into contact with birdlife as well.

For birding trips, check out the website http://www. birdwatchingbulgaria.com or contact the Bulgarian Society for the Protection of Birds (http://www.bspb.org).

Hunting and Fishing

Game hunting for red deer, wild goat, wild boar, grouses, pheasants, partridges and hares are available on forestry farms. Likewise, freshwater fishing is done on farms in the Balkan range. There are chalets and hunters´ lodges for accommodation. For more details, please go to http://www. eurohunters.com

Wine Appreciation And Wine Tours

Founded in March 2006, the Bulgarian Wine Society´s purpose is (in their own words) to introduce European standards to the wine-making sector and to stimulate the domestic wine market and guide the consumer in choosing which wines to drink. To this end, they have wine-tasting sessions and other wine-related events. Check out their website for more detail: http://www.bulgarianwinesociety-bg.com

Wineries and travel agencies also conduct wine tours. See http://www.damianitza.bg and http://www.vegena-bg.com.

Culinary Club

A culinary club cheekily called Desperate Housewives has recently been launched in Sofia by the restaurant Vratata/ La Porte. All wannabe and experienced domestic goddesses can look forward to Sunday afternoons at the restaurant with chef Georgi Ermenkov for culinary lessons and exchange. Aspiring Jamie Olivers can call tel: 866 9005.

The Black Sea Coast

Popular with locals and tourists alike, the Black Sea coast boasts stretches of lovely beaches and competing resorts like Albena, Slunchev Bryag (better known as Sunny Beach to English-speakers) and Zlatni Pyasutsi (Golden Sands). As with all beach resorts, watersports facilities are a dime a dozen, as are nightclubs and other nightlife staples. With all the tourists around, there are also abundant pickpockets and ladies offering male tourists social services. Naysayers complain that these Vegas-like resort hotels are lacking in soul. If you favour something more quaint, head off to Nesebur or Sozopol instead. The Black Sea coast is becoming dangerously overbuilt and hopefully, the building restrictions suggested can be effectively put in place.

SPORTS

Tennis courts, squash courts, indoor and outdoor swimming pool, gyms and fitness centres are available in most cities for working out the after effects of too much *kavarmas* and *kebapchetas*. Those who need to reward themselves after a work-out by quaffing beer will be pleased to know they can do so with like-minded people, the Hash Hound Harriers (http://www.sofiahash.org).

In Sofia, most of the major hotels have pools which are open to the public for a fee, while Olympic-size pools can be found only in some sports complexes such as Spartak (near the Yuzhen Park) and Dianabad. Plovdiv residents have the Plovdiv Sports Complex, the largest in Eastern Europe.

Golf isn't the most popular sport in Bulgaria at the moment, although it is developing in the last few years. As at 2007, there are three courses—in Ihtiman, Sliven and in the village of Ravno Pole near Sofia. Don't be surprised if young boys pop out of the blues offering golf balls for sale on the green. New courses are opening up around the Black Sea region and in Bansko.

With the fantastic mountain ranges, summer sees a lot of enthusiastic hikers heading for them. The more adventurous go in for more extreme sports (see below). Couch potatoes drive up to the foothills and have picnics there, while others

(usually the older generation) clamber around with plastic bags picking herbs.

In winter, the mountains change hats and play hosts to winter sports enthusiasts such as skiing and snowboarding. Do heed the advice and warnings issued about avalanches, and watch out for inconsiderate dare-devils. The favourite skiing resorts are Bansko, Borovets and Pamporovo, while the Vitosha mountain offers the advantage of being only half an hour´s drive away from Sofia. Bansko is Bulgaria´s newest and most fashionable ski resort, situated at an altitude of

Bulgaria has several resorts with good ski slopes.

936 m (3,070 ft), while Borovets is the oldest and largest resort (situated at an altitude of 1,350 m or 4,430 ft). Aleko Ski Centre on Mt. Vitosha is the highest ski resort in Bulgaria at 1, 800m (5,900 ft). Pamporovo resort lays claim to being the sunniest ski resort in Bulgaria and the southernmost of all European ski resorts. It stands at 1,650 m (5,412 ft) in the heart of the Rhodope mountains.

Ice skating is attracting a lot more attention these days though since the Bulgarian ice dance pair, Albena Denkova and Maxim Staviski, won the World Championships in Calgary in 2006 and Tokyo in 2007. In Sofia, Bansko and Haskov, there are skating rinks in winter. Two very accessible skating rinks in Sofia are situated next to the NDK and in front of the Ivan Vasov theatre (a particularly charming location).

Equestrian enthusiasts can go horse-riding in the Pirin, Rhodope and Strandja mountains. In Sofia, horse-riding is available at the Han Asparuh Equestrian Centre in the Ovcha Kupel district and in Boris´ Garden. On some weekends, ponies wait patiently for their young riders in the Yuzhen Park as well.

Sea sports such as wind-surfing, waterskiing and diving are on offer on the Black Sea coast.

Extreme Sports

More challenging pursuits are also available: paragliding, white-water rafting, rock-climbing, canyoning (canyoneering to the Americans), motorcycle tours, quad biking, caving and bungee jumping. A word of caution: make sure your insurance covers extreme sports. When caving, be aware that after a heavy downpour, your exit may be blocked by instant lakes forming.

To check out what, how and where you can give your adrenalin a boost, go to websites www. verticalworldbg. com, www.rotor.bg, www.sky-jet.com, www.motoroads.com, www.adventurenetbg.com and www.zigzagbg.com.

Spectator Sports

Football is the national favourite. The top teams such as Levski Sofia and Lokomotiv Plovdiv play in Champions League and UEFA cup tournaments, and the matches betweent the various Bulgarian clubs are adrenalin-filled occasions for the spectators.

There are other spectator sports like volleyball, basketball, boxing, wrestling, karate and track and field events, but they don´t have the same kind of following that football has.

GETTING AROUND

Travelling by car is obviously the most convenient, as you can go wherever and whenever you want, while booking tours

through the travel agencies saves you the hassle of poring over maps and booking accommodation yourself.

There are also modern coach services operating between the major cities and if in season, to the resorts.

Hemus Air operates domestic flights between Sofia and Varna and Sofia and Bourgas.

Bulgarian State Railways does travel to most towns, but you will have to contend with the (lack of) speed. To reach the more remote areas, travel by bus is necessary. If you don't speak Bulgarian or don't have a Bulgarian with you, it will be a great adventure to travel this way. If you're game to try it, the *Rough Guide* is highly recommended to show you the ins and outs.

ESCAPING ABROAD

Although the country is rich with attractions, the nascent tourist industry, with its still developing infrastructure and erratic level of service, causes the more particular foreign residents and locals to go on overseas vacations. Things are expected to improve with the signing of a memorandum in

April 2007 to set up a Confederation of Bulgarian Tourism, to unite the hitherto large number of tourism bodies into a coherent organisation.

In the meantime, the people who want something different from what Bulgaria has to offer escape overseas. Nearby favourites are Greece and Cyprus, but as it takes only about 2-4 hours flight to get to most of Western Europe, vacationing in other parts of Europe is popular.

By March 2007, there were significantly more flights operated by low-cost airlines: My Air flies to Bologna three times a week, to Venice four times a week; Germanwings flies to and from Cologne three times a week; SkyEurope six times a week to Vienna and Wizz Air flies to Rome thrice in a week. Summers also see an onslaught of more flights, not only to and from Sofia, but Bourgas as well.

SOCIAL WORK
Giving Your Time To A Worthy Cause
There are many NGOs and charitable organisations in Bulgaria, but foreigners tend to be hampered by the lack of command of the language. But there are two places where you can volunteer your time, even if you haven´t quite grasped the intricacies of Bulgarian:

International Womens´ Club (IWC) in Sofia
The IWC in Sofia has a host of activities organised by sub-groups such as the Baby Group, Patchwork-Handicraft Group, Bridge group, Book Club, Scrap book Club, German Conversation Group, English Conversation Group and so on. Apart from organising the activities mentioned above, the IWC is actively involved in charity work. The IWC Charity Foundation funds projects that support or provide assistance to marginalised communities of Bulgarian society such as orphans, the elderly, women and the disabled. The IWC organises an annual Christmas Bazaar which is its major fundraising event of the year.

For more information, see the IWC website at htp://www.IWC-sofia.com or email: iwc_communications@yahoo.co.uk

One Life Charity

This charity focuses on helping children with life-shortening or life-threatening diseases. Their website is http://www.onelifebulgaria.org

Sharing Business Experience

If you´re a business professional and would like to share your knowledge and impart advice to young Bulgarian students, the Bulgarian Business Leaders Forum (which works in association with the Prince of Wales International Business Leaders Forum) organises master classes and other activities to this end. For more information on how you can participate, see http://www.bblf.bg

LEARNING THE LANGUAGE

CHAPTER 8

'If the Romans had been obliged to learn Latin,
they would never have found time to conquer the world'.
—Heinrich Heine (1797–1856), German critic and poet

PERHAPS THE SAME COULD BE SAID of the Bulgarian language. For a foreigner who isn´t a Belarusian, Kazakh, Macedonian, Russian or Serbian, the difficulty lies in first having to learn a whole new alphabet, Cyrillic, even before learning vocabulary and grammar. Being confronted with signs you cannot read isn´t very reassuring. For people coming from a Romance language background, reading Cyrillic for the first time feels like reading a text after a vicious virus has fouled up your computer; there are some familiar letters like ´a´, ´m´, ´c´ and ´g´, but they don´t seem to form words you can identify. You see around you signs stating ´**Р е с т о р а н т**´ and wonder what ´pectopaht´ means, only to find out that it´s actually ´Restorant´ (yes, restaurant). Or you might wonder why so many shops have signs screaming tramp! (´HOBO!´), but it´s Cyrillic for ´N-O-V-O´, which means ´New!´

Nerve-wracking though it may seem at first, coming to grips with the alphabet is much easier once you´ve been in the country for a few months. Surrounded by Cyrillic, the initial strangeness wears away and you´ll be surprised at how quickly you can read words, even if you have no idea what it means. This is already an enormous advantage, as it enables you to read road signs, for example. If you can read Cyrillic, jot down or memorise words you don't understand and ask a Bulgarian later. There are also many words which sounds similar or are

exactly the same as English, French or German words, so once you can read Cyrillic, you´ll recognise words meaning restaurant, efficient, potential and visa. Sometimes a familiar sounding word doesn´t have the same meaning as in English though. The famous folk festival *Pirin Pee* means 'Pirin Sings' and has nothing to do with biological functions.

If you´re living in the country for a period of time, it´s worth picking up some Bulgarian, as any effort on your part will be warmly embraced. It also makes you feel less insecure, being able to ask your way around and understand instructions. Apart from the fact that Bulgarian is now an official EU language, the Cyrillic alphabet is still used by a whopping 224 million people in Russia, Ukraine, Belarus, Bulgaria, Macedonia, Montenegro, Serbia and Bosnia (although the Latin alphabet is also used in Montenegro, Serbia and Bosnia). In some Central Asian countries, Cyrillic is used as well. Good reasons to learn Cyrillic if you intend to travel to these countries.

THE CYRILLIC ALPHABET

Upper and lower case	Pronunciation
А, а	a as in hat
Б, б	b as in baby
В, в	v as in vein
Г, г	g as in good
Д, д	d as in dog
Е, е	e as in pen
Ж, ж	Zh like the `s´ in vision
З, з	z as in zebra
И, и	i as in ink
Й, й	y as in yes
К, к	k as in kite
Л, л	l as in lemon
М, м	m as in man
Н, н	n as in now
О, о	o as in off
П, п	p as in pat
Р, Р	r as in ran
С, с	s as in soon
Т, т	t as in train
У, у	u as in mule
Ф, ф	f as in friend
Х, х	ch as in `loch´ (easier for German speakers!)
Ц, ц	ts as in bats
Ч, ч	ch as in chess
Ш, ш	sh as in shut
Щ, щ	sht like the ending of `pushed´
Ъ, ъ	u like in urn
Ь, ь	this letter is not pronounced but softens the following consonant
Ю, ю	yu as in you
Я, я	ya as in yahoo

THE HISTORY

With the aim of spreading Christianity, two Thessaloniki-based missionary brothers, Cyril (827–869) and Methodius (825–885) developed a Slavonic alphabet to translate the

Bible. The two brothers came up with the Glagolic alphabet in the year 855, an artistic predecessor to Cyrillic. It was the disciples of Cyril and Methodius who simplified the ornate Glagolic into what we know as Cyrillic today. The disciples called the alphabet Cyrillic to honour Cyril.

Both Cyril and Methodius were canonised in Eastern Orthodoxy as 'equal-to-apostles' and were included in the universal Roman Catholic Church Calendar by Pope Leo XIII in 1880.

Bulgarians are immensely proud of their alphabet and 24 May is a national holiday called the Day of Bulgarian Enlightenment and Culture and of the Slavonic Alphabet. Bulgarians are also lobbying for 'EVRO' (what Bulgarians call the Euro) to be written in Cyrillic on the Euro banknotes.

Cyrillic is seen as intrinsically Bulgarian, as it developed and spread mostly within the territory of the then First Bulgarian Kingdom. Given that these areas are nowadays within the borders of its neighbours, Macedonians, Czechs, Slovakians, Ukrainians, Russians and Greeks take issue with Bulgaria´s claim that Bulgaria is the birthplace of Cyrillic, although it´s best not to doubt Bulgarians´ right to claim Cyrillic as their own while in Bulgaria.

CYRILLIC AS AN EU ALPHABET

With Bulgaria´s entry into the European Union, Cyrillic has become the EU´s third official alphabet, after Latin and Greek. Translators are rubbing their hands in glee in view of the potential increase in business, not least in having to translate the copious EU documents. The EU directorate-general for translation alone needs about 60 full-time translators for each language. EU computers use Unicode, a character-encoding system that has no problems dealing with the multitude of world alphabets, but difficulties are faced by translators as some EU terminology simply has no Bulgarian equivalent. Goodness, what should `flexsecurity´ be in Bulgarian?

> Most road signs and location maps in public areas are solely in Cyrillic, which makes an ability to read Cyrillic so critical.

Returning The Favour

Bulgaria is not obliged to display signs in Latin, but the country intends to do so. Finances aside, the task of having Latin signs causes migraines. Many Cyrillic letters have no Latin equivalent, or various possibilites. The result is, till now, a free-for-all transliteration. You therefore find, for example, the ´name of the city by the Danube variously spelt Ruse, Russe or Rousse. Nikolay Vassilev, minister for state administration and administrative reform, therefore launched a transliteration system created by linguists to standardise the transliteration of Bulgarian names into the Latin alphabet. The new spelling is now compulsory for state institutions but it will take years before it is fully used by the average Todorov or Todorova in the street. Just look at how far the German spelling reform of 1996 has progressed (or even regressed).

CYRILLIC AND MODERN TECHNOLOGY

The good news is that SMSing (and often Internet communication) are done using Latin text interfaces. Young Bulgarians have improvised a new Latin-based alphabet, so once you master some Bulgarian, you can still SMS with the Latin alphabet. There are Cyrillic keyboards for computers.

Samples of Cyrillic signs. The top picture means 'PULL' while the bottom picture shows the name for MacDonald's.

Difficulties

Learning a new letter from scratch may be difficult, but having to consciously remember not to be tricked by `false friends´ (B, P, C and X) really puts people used to Latin alphabet into a tizzy. And just when you start patting yourself on the back for having mastered all 30 letters, you discover that handwritten (or cursive) letters can look extremely different from the Cyrillic block letters but resemble (but aren´t the same) as Latin alphabets. Confused? Take `m´ and `g´, for example. They are not Latin `m´and `g´, but `т´ and `д´ (i.e. Latin `t´ and `d´). The handwritten form is sometimes used in advertisements, so be prepared for a test of your cognitive abilities in Bulgaria. To paraphrase Heinrich Heine, if terrorists have had to learn Bulgarian, there wouldn´t have been a need to invade Afghanistan.

If you want to have a look at what cursive Cyrillic looks like, go to http://plovdivguide.com/thingstoknow/1/cyrillic/?lang_id = 1

Bulgarian, like French and German, has nouns which are male, female or neutral, but there is no fixed pattern to follow. Wolves, nightingales, carrots and museums are all male. Monkeys, sheep, pears and machines are female, while dogs, seeds, letters and cabbages are neutral. Surprisingly, child, boy and girl are also neutral. The plural of a noun is formed by attaching endings to the noun; the type of ending depends on the gender of the noun. Bulgarian also distinguishes between formal and informal `you´, so you have to be careful not to use the informal `you´ when speaking to someone senior, a VIP or a total stranger.

These gives you an idea of the grammatical rules of the Bulgarian language, which is admittedly complex. I´ve personally found Bulgarian to be the hardest foreign language of the six or so I´ve grappled with. But if you only want to learn enough for the absolute basics, you won´t have to worry too much about the finer points of Bulgarian.

LEARNING BULGARIAN

As mentioned in the opening paragraph, when you´re surrounded by Bulgarian signs all the time, you start to recognise letters and even whole words faster than you´d dare imagine. So take heart.

Although foreigners living in Sofia can get by without learning the language, you will find that it´s harder to find Bulgarians fluent in English (or any other European language) farther outside the city. If you´re going to be living in Bulgaria for a period of time, learning some Bulgarian will endear you to the locals (you might even get a larger portion when eating in a *mehana*) or at least lessen the chances of your being fleeced by shopkeepers and taken for a (figurative) ride by devious taxi-drivers.

Learning Bulgarian can be done at language schools, with a private tutor or on your own. The latter option has the disadvantage of your not hearing the pronunciation and not being able to ask questions, unless you have a Bulgarian spouse or a good friend who´s willing to take all your persistent questions.

As with all languages, what you learn in school may be very correct, but probably makes you sound like a Martian or an uptight headmaster when trying it out on a pretty girl in the disco. But chatting bravely with the locals is the best way to get the hang of everyday Bulgarian. Making mistakes is common for everyone new to a language and Bulgarians will be so pleased you´re trying that they´ll help you along if you fumble. Watching TV is also useful; you may not understand anything in the beginning but you´ll certainly pick up on the intonation and a feel for the language.

Learn on the Go
A few Bulgarian phrases can be downloaded onto your MP3 player or printed out at: http://www.bbc.co.uk/languages/other/quickfix/bulgarian.shtml

---

Where to go for Bulgarian Courses
- **The Department of Language Learning, Sofia University St. Kliment Ohridski**
  http://www.deo.uni-sofia.bg

- **Alexander Language Schools Franchise**
  http://www.als-alexander.org
- **Mastylo language School, Plovdiv**
  http://www.mastylo.net

NUMBERS
Numbers are thankfully relatively straightforward, compared to, for example, French, where some numbers involve mathematical skills e.g. 96 is *quatre-vingt seize* (4x20 + 16), or German where it's *sechsundneunzig* (six and ninety) instead of a simple *neunzigsechs*. In Bulgarian, 96 is *devetdeset i shesh*, a straightforward ninety and six.

MACEDONIAN LANGUAGE
Bulgaria has never really recovered from the loss of Macedonia and the inability to get back the lands. For many, if not all, Macedonia is Bulgarian and there is therefore no such nonsense as a Macedonian language; the Macedonians speak a Bulgarian dialect, and that's it. The relationship between Macedonia and Bulgaria is like the one between China and Taiwan.

NON-VERBAL COMMUNICATION
When we're not able to communicate in a common language, we depend very much on gestures to bring our message across. Things are fine if gestures have the same meaning in all cultures, but unfortunately they don't. One of the gestures that frequently cause foreigners in Bulgaria to come to grief is the nodding and shaking of heads to mean yes and no. This is of fundamental importance, so it bears repeating: a shake of the head is yes and a nod is no in Bulgaria. But younger Bulgarians may oblige foreigners by doing it 'our' way, resulting in confusion all round. The best is to clearly say *da* for yes, and *ne* for no with your head movements.

You might also want to note that a wave from someone doesn't mean goodbye, but come here.

The Non-Verbal Meaning Of Verbal Communication

A Bulgarian may be having a discussion with you in fluent English, but sometimes you should not take what he says too literally. Bulgarians who are not prepared to make a commitment about something, or find it difficult to say no to you may prattle in a roundabout way. Don´t insist `Get to the point!´ Or they may actually say something like "I called my colleague but I can´t get hold of her. I´ll call you back when I´ve talked to her". If the person doesn´t call you back, don´t call her every half hour to see if she´s managed to reach her colleague, unless it´s a matter of life and death. The promise to call you back is as dependable as when a gorgeous guy tells a not-so-gorgeous girl "I´ll call you". It´s a statement with no real intention; just a polite way of escaping from an uncomfortable situation.

DOING BUSINESS AND THE ECONOMY

'So, next time you hit a pothole on the road, just try to concentrate on Bulgaria's bright future.'
—Plamen Doudov, in his article 'Bulgarian Regions Hit the EU Road' in *Vagabond* magazine, February 2007

WITH BULGARIA´S ENTRY INTO THE EUROPEAN UNION, there is a heightened interest in doing business in the country, spurred by the belief that it is now easier with EU rules and regulations in place. While this is true to a certain extent, hiccups can be expected now and then, as the country has so recently joined the EU. Old habits also die hard, which rules and regulations cannot change overnight. But factors like the low cost of labour and corporate-friendly taxes make doing business in Bulgaria very attractive.

The country´s tumultuous history has coloured the perceptions and attitudes of the people, and you will be able to see it playing out in the business world as well.

ATTITUDES AND WORK CULTURE

Bulgaria´s history of being occupied by a foreign power and their many years as a country cut off from the rest of Europe have left the people harbouring a general mistrust of foreigners. Perhaps because of this mistrust, society is rather collectivist, as is mentioned earlier in Chapter 3. For example, a collectivist mentality can pose problems in areas like quality management; good service tends to be given only to those who belong to one´s own group.

Cross cultural expert Prof. Michael Minkov said that Bulgarians are fatalists, and tend to think that what happens to them is not their own doing and that´s why they don´t wear seat belts in cars, or helmets on construction sites and why they think that if they´re late, it´s not their fault. This might sound a bit harsh, but there certainly is a sort of recklessness in many Bulgarians.

According to psychologist Ivan Igov, Bulgaria´s years under a totalitarian regime has also left the people with a behavioural condition which psychologists call ´learned helplessness´. People who are not in a position to make any real changes in their lives become apathetic. Such people then expect someone else to make all the decisions, especially people in authority. They wait to take instructions and orders from above, and are at a lost when asked to make suggestions or brain storm. I´ve witnessed this characteristic myself once at a conference for members of the Bar. The dynamic lady president of the Bar Association asked for suggestions from members on legal reform or comments, after speeches were made by top officials. A very loud silence followed. My experience of my legal brethrens had always been that it was difficult to *stop* them talking, and not vice versa. So this teenager-at-a-first-date type of shyness was a real surprise.

Foreigners may also find their colleagues and employees lacking in the ability to plan long-term. Someone from a Chamber of Commerce cited me the example of a Bulgarian exporter blithely signing a contract to supply strawberries without being certain he could source the amount contracted. He only started looking for the goods after signing the contract. When he failed to find the required quantity, he simply told the importer that he could cancel the contract.

After the years of socialism where people were paid a fixed amount, irrespective of how much they worked (or not), many Bulgarian employees also do not attend to work with a hair-on-fire sense of urgency.

Foreigners in advertising have also had to struggle with the Bulgarians´ disinterest. In an interview with *Sofia Echo*, Nick Saunders (CEO of Golden Pages Bulgaria, a classified business directory) commented on having to overcome the ´I don´t need to advertise´ attitude. The general attitude is ´I´ve survived for 20 years without advertising, why should

I do it now?´and `Who are you to tell me what I should do?´. He also found that there was a lack of long-term planning and strategy; the focus was on making profits and run and never mind about the future.

Bulgarians are not strong on punctuality, so this can be very trying on businessmen used to things running like Swiss timepieces.

Attitude Towards Female Colleagues

It is not surprising to find a male (especially if he´s older) sounding a bit sharp with a female colleague or giving her a withering look if he disapproved of what she´s saying. Sometimes the males may make what sounds like sexist comments too, but it´s generally accepted by people in patriarchal societies.

BUSINESS ETIQUETTE
Business Attire

Business suits are the norm for men and women. Women are advised to avoid loud colours and distracting jewellery, although they should appear well-groomed. Casual wear is not recommended, not even on Fridays.

Meeting & Greeting

It may take some time to fix an appointment as many senior executives have not yet been able to exorcise themselves from the Communist era bureaucracy. When the date of the appointment nears, it´s useful to confirm the date and time again. Don´t bother arranging a meeting in July and August as it´s summer vacation time. The Christmas and New Year period is also a bad time for business meetings.

The way to greet Bulgarian business people is no different from greeting other British, French or German ones. A handshake and a `Dobro utro´ (Good Morning), `Dobur den' (Good Day) or `Dobur vecher´ (Good evening) while making eye contact is the norm. A word of caution for ladies who are greeting a man: don´t go overboard with the `eye contact´ advice; look a person in the eyes to avoid appearing shifty or impolite, but avoid staring too fixedly at a man for too long as it may give him wrong ideas! Make it a point to shake hands with everyone at the meeting.

If you know someone´s title (e.g. Dr./Professor), do use it. If not, address a man as `Gospodin´(Mr) and a lady as Gospozha´(Mrs/Mdm) followed by the person´s surname. Gospozha is used whether the lady is married or single; there is no equivalent of the neutral `Ms´. It´s not common to go on first-name basis in Bulgaria among business partners.

Most Bulgarian businessmen speak fluently English, German or French (or even a few European languages), but if you can manage a few Bulgarian words or phrases, it will be a brownie point for you.

Business Cards

At meetings, business cards are exchanged, so make sure you have plenty with you. There isn´t any specific way of handing out or receiving business cards, as is the case in some Asian countries. However, common courtesy (and common sense) dictates that you have a look at the card to show an interest in the person instead of shoving it unceremoniously into your back pocket without a second glance. Obviously, it´s rude to use someone´s business card to scribble information or another person´s telephone number on.

For your own business card, you would want to add your academic qualification or title on it. If your company was founded more than twenty years ago, add the founding date on your card. Foreigners in Bulgaria often have both sides of their business card printed; one in English and the other in Bulgarian.

Business Gifts

Corporate gifts like leather bound diaries and other quality stationery with your company logo would make suitable gifts for business partners.

At Meetings and Negotiations

Bulgarians are not famous for their punctuality, so don´t be surprised if the meeting does not start on time.

As mentioned above, Bulgarians are often cautious when dealing with foreigners. It takes a few meetings before they get down to business, so don´t fly into the country with a contract expecting them to sign it at the first meeting. Don´t feel frustrated, either, if after a few meetings, you feel as if you´ve achieved nothing concrete. You actually have, in Bulgarian terms; you have built up a relationship with your Bulgarian counterparts, which is an important aspect of business dealings for Bulgarians.

When you finally get down to discussing business proper, focus on facts and statistics and avoid too much `talk´. Remember that eye contact conveys sincerity to Bulgarians. At no time should you slip into a more casual mode; formality and professionalism are highly valued characteristics. Don´t try to impose a time schedule on when discussions should end and decision-making done. Bulgarians like to digest the information at their own pace, and will not be comfortable making a decision until they´ve thought through all the facts and figures.

If you find your business counterparts beating around the bush and not giving very direct answers to your questions, chances are they are not prepared to commit themselves. Don´t persist with the same questions; they will give you an answer when they´re ready, or you can try to ask indirect questions to get a feel of the direction the discussion is going.

Meetings will usually be followed by a business lunch or dinner. Bulgarians are very hospitable, so be ready to be wined and dined. Brown bag lunches while continuing with negotiations will fill Bulgarians with horror. You can expect a rather protracted lunch (starting around 1pm) or dinner (starting around 7pm).

Holidays and Other Celebrations with Colleagues

Many foreigners are struck (no doubt delighted, too) by the number of non-working days in Bulgaria. It isn´t just the number of official holidays *per se*; the government usually declares an extra day off when a public holiday falls near a weekend. In 2007, for example, 1st May (Labour Day) fell on a Tuesday, so Monday was declared a public holiday. 24th May (Day of Slavonic Literacy) conveniently landed on a Thursday, so Friday was declared a non-working day. Sept 6 (Unification Day) also fell on a Thursday, so it was another long weekend.

Every August, everyone disappears on holiday, if they haven't already gone in July.

On working days, there are yet more possibilities to down tools and celebrate. Name days are celebrated with a serious purpose, so whoever is celebrating his/her Name Day will bring chocolates for the colleagues or better yet, something alcoholic as well. If you happen to have a first name which does not have a Name Day in Bulgaria, don't even think you can escape the ritual. You have to do the same thing on your birthday. If you're in a senior position, it's a nice gesture to buy your staff lunch.

Some Name Days

2 Jan	Silvia
18 Apr	Viktor, Viktoria
7 Jun	Valeria, Valeri
26 Jun	David
18 Jul	Emil, Emilian
26 Aug	Adrian, Adriana
14 Nov	Filip, Filipa
6 Dec	Nikola, Nikolay, Nina

On 8 March, you might notice that your female colleagues are specially dolled up and there's an air of excitement. Yes, it's International Women's Day and Bulgarian women are traditionally given flowers (reminder: odd number of stems!) by men on this day. The practice in Bulgaria actually stems from communist days, though, when this day celebrated the `heroic women workers´.

At Christmas and Easter, it's also a nice gesture to bring something for your staff or colleagues. Don't forget the cleaning lady and driver.

THE ECONOMY

With the fall of communism, Bulgaria´s path to democracy and a market economy was a long, hard struggle. The political upheavals in the early 1990s, the slow pace of reforms and rampant corruption after the fall of communism ensured that by 1996, the country´s economy was teethering on the brink of collapse. There was little choice left for the Union of Democratic Forces government elected in April 1997 but to swallow the IMF-imposed bitter pill. An economic austerity programme was introduced, the lev was pegged to the Deutschmark to rein in galloping inflation and an IMF standby agreement was negotiated.

During ex-king Simeon II´s premiership (2001-2005), the country pushed tenaciously on with market reforms. Growth was achieved, unemployment fell and inflation was under control, although incomes and living standards did not rise quickly enough for the impatient populace.

In April 2005, Bulgaria signed an EU accession treaty, bringing renewed hope for the people, and generated an interest in the country by investors. Bulgaria joined the EU in January 2007. With Bulgaria´s accession to the EU, foreign direct investment is expected to increase. What may hinder prospective investors from taking the plunge are corruption, the cumbersome and confusing regulations, a weak judiciary, organised crime and the insufficient protection of intellectual property rights.

Although Bulgaria had a strong agricultural tradition, the service industry has grown very quickly. By 2006, services accounted for about 54.3 per cent of the GDP, compared to 32.1 per cent for industry and a mere 13.6 per cent for agriculture. Official figures do not, however, take into account a thriving grey economy, which is estimated to be between 30 to 40 per cent of GDP.

Foreign Direct Investments (FDI)

The largest foreign investor in Bulgaria from 1992 to 2006 was Austria with an investment of three billion Euros, followed by the Netherlands (1.5 billion Euros) and Greece (1.2 billion Euros). The other big investors are the United

Kingdom, Germany, Italy, Hungary, Czech Republic, Belgium/ Luxembourg, Switzerland and the United States. Most of the investments were in the service sector such as financial services, real estate, trade, telecommunications, transport and tourism.

Foreign direct investment from January to August 2008 totalled 2,980 Euros, a drop from 4,154 Euros in the same period in 2007. In that period, Austria was the largest investor (13.9%), followed by the Netherlands (11.3%) and Germany (10.7%).

The common refrain of foreign investors is that they are scared off by the corruption and bureaucracy. The US ambassador, John Beyrle, was refreshingly honest and said that American companies were discouraged from investing in Bulgaria by factors such as the lack of a skilled labour force, the spotty enforcement of copyrights and intellectual property laws and an environment that was not encouraging for the small and medium-sized companies. They were also put off by long administrative delays and obstacles, which were excuses for demanding bribes and kickbacks. The German ambassador, Michael Geier, likewise commented that German investors complained about the lack of a qualified workforce and the lethargic pace of decision-making procedures at the local level.

The first six months of being a European Union member were clouded by corruption scandals and contract killings; two ministers resigned and two deputy ministers were fired in June 2007. All these certainly didn´t augur well for the country´s reputation.

Businessmen from countries which are signatories to the OECD Convention on Combating Bribery of Foreign Public Officials have to be careful not to fall foul of legislations in their own countries that make it illegal to pay bribes to foreign public officials. Doing business in a country where corruption is rife would certainly be walking a tight-rope.

To be fair, Bulgaria suffers badly from image problem-more than it deserves. A survey by Ernst and Young in October 2006 which polled 200 senior corporate executives world-wide found that Bulgaria´s image among foreign investors was weaker than the actual foreign investments it attracted. Bulgaria in fact ranked second (after Romania) among some seven south-eastern European countries in terms of FDI. What made Bulgaria attractive was its low labour costs and corporate tax. According to those polled, the areas in which Bulgaria had to improve on were its transport and communication infrastructures, its political, legal and regulatory environment, compliance with European economic regulation standards and its mind-boggling administrative procedures.

Taxes

Bulgaria has very agreeable tax rates: corporate tax is a flat 10 per cent and the top income tax rate of 24 per cent is low, compared against the rates of some other European countries. In November 2007, legislation to introduce a flat income tax rate of 10 per cent went through a first reading in parliament.

Individuals currently pay progressive tax on their income at a rate of 10–24 per cent. The employer deducts income tax and national insurance from the employees´ salaries at source.

Bulgaria has signed Double Tax Prevention Treaties with many countries including Austria, Belgium, Canada, China, Denmark, France, Germany, India, Italy, the Netherlands and UK. The treaties take precedence over the Bulgarian Income Tax Ordinance.

Labour Costs

With an average national monthly wage of 400 leva, labour costs is definitely not a cause for concern for potential investors.

Strengths and Shortcomings of the Labour Market

The years under a communist regime has developed certain characteristics which is still prevalent in the Bulgarian labour market. Rigid working hours and lack of motivation is still common, as employees have had little exposure to competition and meritocracy. Management is still primarily

top-down, rather than consultative, and often plagued by cronyism. Many foreign managers I spoke to often mention the lack of initiative of the local staff, too.

Bulgaria has certainly suffered from a brain drain, with an estimated one million people having emigrated since 1990. This, together with an education system that is not yet synergised with the practical demands of the market, resulted in a shortage of specialists in certain industries such as information technology, engineering and banking. According to EUROSTAT statistics reported in the local media in 2007, Bulgaria is among the countries in Europe having low computer literacy, with nearly 70 per cent of the Bulgarian men and 69 per cent of the women lacking in computer skills. This high level of computer illiteracy is not evident at first glance, as the government agencies and many leading companies have well contructed and informative websites in English, and business people are often very computer savvy. The country is certainly facing the problem of digital divide.

But this is not to say that Bulgaria is totally lacking in competent labour; Bulgarians are strong in mathematics and many of the younger Bulgarians speak at least one foreign language (English, German or French) fluently, so with the appropriate training and incentives, they will be able to do the job, and well. The heads of a European bank and a five-star hotel confirmed that their staff were able to perform well, after undergoing training, even though they had no banking/hotel experience at all when they started.

Employers are hampered by laws that prevent them from employing foreigners, such as the rules that foreigners may not make up more than 10 per cent of a company's total employees, and that foreigners can only be hired if the position had been offered to a Bulgarian first. If no Bulgarian applied for it, the employer must apply for permission from the National Employment Agency and pay a fee before the job can be given to a foreigner.

The Impact of EU Accession

The common fear is that EU accession will see an increase of emigration of able and willing Bulgarians to richer European countries. But perhaps EU accession could actually bring Bulgarians who have already been working overseas to return, as international companies head-hunt overseas Bulgarians to take up senior management positions back in Bulgaria on expatriate terms.

There is also an expectation that overhead costs for businesses will climb as Bulgarian companies comply with EU standards and regulations. Initial higher costs notwithstanding, investors see the positive side of EU accession as the rules and regulations for doing business will be more familiar European ones than the previous guessing games.

The potholes that Bulgaria has to circumvent on the road to a bright European future are the lack of administrative and technical capacity to absorb EU funds, its creaking infrastructure and the oft-mentioned organised crime, corruption and a judicial system that urgently needs reform.

Unlike many of the EU-15 countries, the more recent EU member countries like the Czech Republic, Hungary, Poland and Slovakia have opened up their labour markets to Bulgarians and Romanians. When these countries joined the EU in 2004, they saw an exodus of their people to the

EU 15 countries. So with Bulgaria and Romania now EU members, professionals and specialists like engineers, IT specialists, doctors, nurses and mid-wives would find a plethora of job offers there, with the only possible obstacle being language.

Organised Crime and the Grey Economy

An article published in the New York Times in 2009 said that the European Union (EU) found Bulgaria lagging in tackling fraud, corruption and organized crime since joining the union in 2007. As a result, the European Commission decided to freeze 50 million Euros of subsidies intended to help Bulgaria make the necessary economic reforms.

Bulgaria is also plagued by a substantial grey economy. There is massive hiding of revenues especially in sectors such as construction, tourism, trade and finances, according to the chairman of the Bulgarian Industrial Association. Common practices include under-invoicing and under-declaring of prices for property, shares and assets sales.

Infrastructure

The level of FDI in the country could probably be much higher, had there been a better infrastructure in place, especially the transport network. Given Bulgaria´s strategic location between Europe and Asia, and the Baltic Sea and the Mediterranean Sea, there is a money tree waiting to be shaken.

Socio-economic development and dependable infra-structure in Bulgaria are currently concentrated in and around the cities of Sofia, Plovdiv, Varna, Burgas, Rousse, Pleven and Stara Zagora. The other parts of Bulgaria which are without a big city in its vicinity are characterised by a lack of infrastructure and public services, insufficient public transport, lack of economic activities and the resultant low employment and emigration to the cities.

The hope lies in the five Pan-European Transport Corridors which will criss-cross Bulgaria, and enhance the country´s location between Europe and Asia, and the Baltic and the Mediterranean Seas.

The Concentration of the Economy

Sofia, the capital, is where most of the country's economy is focused. The capital, blessed with developed infrastructure, qualified residents and accessibility to and from other countries, sees a high level of economic growth and about 15 per cent higher salaries compared to other cities like Plovdiv, Varna, Stara Zagora and Bourgas. The downside is that the city's infrastructure is severely stretched, the most obvious sign being the horrible jams and lack of parking spaces.

Plovdiv is the second largest city by population, but economically, Varna and Bourgas are doing better.

Varna, in particular, has been playing catch-up in an impressive way. Retailers and major companies have taken notice of the little brother in the northeastern corner of the country. A port city which is strategically located on one of the Pan-European Transport corridors, with an airport that has seen increasing traffic, there is little doubt that Varna's future is bright.

Bureaucracy

The bane of foreigners and locals alike, and something which has not gone away with EU accession, the bureaucratic jungle is not expected to improve anytime soon. The miserly salaries public servants get encourage them to squeeze some leva out of people they deem beholden to them (which you are if you are trying to get a work permit, for example). Even if it's not bribes they are after, there isn't much motivation, and once you've seen the decrepit offices they have to work in, you'd understand why. Whether they're efficient or not, the salary and work environment remain the same, so why bother?

That leaves you facing dour types who will ask you for all sorts of documents, with different officers asking for different things, or worse, the same officer asking for different things on different days.

Corruption and Nepotism

Bulgaria ranked 71 with a score of 3.8 in Transparency International's 2009 Corruption Perception Index. The three pole position countries, New Zealand, Denmark and

Singapore, had scores of 9.2–9.4 (out of 10). Romania scored 3.8 and Poland 5.0.

The collectivist behaviour mentioned above also means there is a tendency to give jobs to relatives and friends, so someone may be in a senior position, not because of abilities, but because of connections. Human Resource managers should be aware of this when looking at a very impressive CV of a candidate.

Management Positions Available

There is a huge need for additional management competence, so I encourage every Bulgarian leader to establish more business schools for the young and bright students so that they can stay in [the] country......Bulgaria has its strengths in education and one of the strong sides, according to me, are the mathematical skills and the language schools all over Bulgaria. Here languages are learnt as a mother tongue, and this gives a true competitive advantage to the Bulgarian labour market. Finding highly qualified staff is very difficult and there is still the tendency for such people to go and work abroad. Our approach is to hire rather inexperienced but well intentioned young people from the university and train them.

—Ullrich G. Schubert, CEO, BNP Paribas Bulgaria,
in an interview with the *Sofia Echo* (May 25-31, 2007 issue)

During the annual Rose Festival, Kazanluk celebrates its harvest of the best oil-producing rose. Celebrations include singing, dancing and ritual rose-picking by children and adults wearing traditional Bulgarian dress.

Built in 13th century, the Church of Christ Pantocrator in the ancient city of Nessebar remains one of the best examples of period architecture in European history. The church, along with the entire island and historical structures, is a UNESCO World Heritage Site.

The Tsar Osvoboditel statue overlooking the National Assembly in Sofia. The monument was erected in honour of Russian Emperor Alexander II who liberated Bulgaria of Ottoman rule during the Russo-Turkish War of 1877-78.

НАРОДЕН Т

One of Sofia's most important landmarks, the Ivan Vasov National Theatre was designed by Austrians and built in 1907. Initially just called the National Theatre, it was later named after the prominent Bulgarian poet, novelist and playwright.

Knaz Alexander Street in Plovdiv's city centre.
Next to Sofia, the picturesque town is Bulgaria's
second-largest city, home to many parks, gardens,
museums and archaeological monuments.

FAST FACTS

CHAPTER 10

'Seven years are a long period, but I think you never
get accustomed [to a new country]. I discover new things
about Bulgaria and Bulgarians every day......'
—Ullrich G. Schubert, CEO, BNP Paribas Bulgaria

Official Name
The Republic of Bulgaria

Capital
Sofia (550 m above sea level)

Flag
Three horizontal bands of equal width, in white (top band), green and red.

National anthem
Mila Rodino (O Motherland Most Dear)
The anthem is based on a tune and lyrics written by Tsvetan Radoslavov in 1885. He composed them on his way to the battlefield during the Serbo-Bulgarian War. Adopted as Bulgaria's national anthem in 1964, there have been numerous revisions to the original by Radoslavov. For full text, see Chapter 2.

Time
GMT +2

Telephone country code
+359

Main City Codes
(add 0 in front if dialing from within Bulgaria)

SOFIA	2
Blagoevgrad	73
Bourgas	56
Dobrich	58
Gabrovo	66
Haskovo	38
Kyustendil	78
Lovech	68
Pazardjik	34
Pernik	76
Pleven	64
Plovdiv	32
Rousse	82
Silistra	86
Sliven	44
Stara Zagora	42
Varna	52
Veliko Tarnovo	62
Vidin	94
Vratsa	92
Yambol	46

Area
Total: 110,993.6 sq. km (42,855 sq. miles)
Land: 110,550 sq. km (42,684 sq. miles)
Water: 443 sq. km (171 sq. miles)

Highest and Lowest Point
Musala (2,925 m/9,596 ft) and Black Sea (0 m)
Lowlands (up to 200 m/656 ft): 31.5 per cent of the country;
mountains (over 600 m/1,969 ft): 27.5 per cent of the country

Major Rivers
Danube, Maritsa, Mesta, Strouma, Iskur and Yantra

Climate
Temperate continental with Black Sea influence in the east

and Mediterranean in the south. Cold winters (average minus 1°C/33.8°F) and hot, dry summers (average 20-22°C /68–71.6°F)

Natural resources
Copper, lead, zinc, bauxite, coal, timber, arable land

Population
7,623,385 (2008 figures)

Ethnic Groups
Bulgarian officialdom avoids making ethnic distinctions. CIA Factbook estimates that the ethnic breakdown is as follows: 83.9 per cent Bulgarians, 9.4 per cent Turks, 4.7 per cent Romas and 2 per cent of others (Macedonians, Armenians, Tatars and Circassians)

Religion
East Orthodox Christians (85 per cent), Muslims (13 per cent), Catholics (1 per cent);

Language
Bulgarian (Cyrillic alphabet)

Government
Bulgaria is a parliamentary democracy, with the Constitution of the Republic (passed in July 1991) as the supreme law of the country.

The legislature is the unicameral Narodno Sabranie (National Assembly) with 240 members who are directly elected every four years (last elections in 2005). The current prime minister is Sergei Stanishev.

The head of the state is the President (currently Georgi Purvanov), who is directly elected every five years (last elections in 2006). Purvanov is serving his second term.

Administrative divisions
28 in total: Blagoevgrad, Bourgas, Dobrich, Gabrovo, Haskovo, Kardjali, Kyustendil, Lovech, Montana, Pazardjik, Pernik,

Pleven, Plovdiv, Razgrad, Rousse, Shumen, Silistra, Sliven, Smolyan, Sofia city, Sofia region, Stara Zagora, Targovishte, Varna, Veliko Tarnovo, Vidin, Vratsa, Yambol

Currency
Lev (plural leva). The currency code is BGN.
1 lev = 100 stotinki
The lev is pegged to the Euro at the exchange rate of 1 lev = 0.51129 Euro. Coins are in the following denominations: 1, 2, 5, 10, 20, 50 stotinki and 1 lev. Notes are denominated in: 2, 5, 10, 20, 50, 100 leva

Gross Domestic Profit (GDP)
Purchasing power parity (PPP): US$90.44 billion (2009 est.)
GDP per capita (PPP): US$12,600 (2009 est.)

Agricultural Products
Fruits, vegetables, tobacco, wine, sunflowers, wheat, barley, sugar beets, livestock

Industries
Electricity, refined petroleum, chemicals (fertilisers, soda, plastics, pharmaceuticals), tobacco, food, beverages, machinery and equipment, base metals, electronics, telecommunications, tourism

Exports
Clothing and footwear, iron and steel, chemicals, plastic and rubber, electricity
Export partners are Italy, Turkey, Germany and Greece

Imports
Machinery and equipment, textiles, chemicals and plastics, crude oil and gas, minerals
Import partners are Germany, Russia, Italy and Turkey

Ports and harbours
Bourgas, Varna, Rousse, Lom, Vidin

Airports

Total: 217
With paved runways: 132
With unpaved runways: 85
Sofia International Airport is the main international airport, but with tourism picking up, Bourgas, Varna and Plovdiv airports are expected to cater to more international flights.

Railways

4,294 km/2,668 miles, mostly standard gauge

FAMOUS PEOPLE

Inventors

John Vincent Atanasoff

Born in New York in 1903 to a Bulgarian immigrant, Atanasoff is the Father of the Computer to Bulgarians. Atanasoff, together with his graduate student, Clifford Berry built the Atanasoff-Berry Computer (ABC) at Iowa State University between 1939 and 1942, although credit for their pioneering work eluded them for a long time. Instead, J. Mauchly and J. Presper Eckert were hailed as the inventors of the first computer, the ENIAC (Electronic Numerical Integrator and Calculator). It was only in a 1973 US court battle between Honeywell and Sperry Rand that it was proven that Mauchly had in fact drawn on Atanasoff´s ABC to built the ENIAC, after visiting Atanasoff´s laboratory and reading his manual.

Carl Djerassi

Djerassi was born in Vienna in 1923 to a Bulgarian father and an Austrian mother. He was the creator of the contraceptive pill, although this was not his primary aim. His childhood was spent in Sofia, before moving later to Vienna and then to the US in 1939, taking up American citizenship in 1945.

Djerassi created a progesterone that could be orally active, the objective of which was to treat menstrual disorders and infertility, and discovered that it could also be used as a contraceptive pill. It was only a decade later that the FDA approved it as a contraceptive and it became the Pill.

Djerassi was also an accomplished author and playwright, publishing five novels, three plays, a book of short stories, an autobiography and a memoir.

Stamen Grigorov
Dr. Grigorov was the one who discovered that a certain strain of bacillus turned milk into yoghurt. Born in the village of Studen Izvor, Bulgaria in 1878, he completed his secondary education in natural sciences in Montpellier, France and medical science in Geneva, Switzerland. It was in Geneva in 1905 that the young Dr. Grigorov made the discovery for which he is best known.

Musicians and Artists
Bulgaria has produced many internationally acclaimed opera singers such as Boris Christoff, Ghena Dimitrova, Nicolai Ghiaurov, Raina Kabaivanska and Anna Tomova-Sintova. Below are write-ups of only two of them, for reasons of space contraints, but they have all performed in top opera houses.

Boris Christoff
In 1914, the city of Plovdiv had a new son who would go on to become a top bass. Although he was a magistrate, his spare time was devoted to singing. It was only in 1942 that he left on a government grant for Italy to study under Riccardo Stracciari. He went on to perform in La Scala, Convent Garden and many other European opera houses. Invited to perform at the Metropolitan Opera in New York in 1950, his appearance was thwarted by the McCarran Immigration Act, which prevented citizens of the Soviet bloc from entering the US.

Christoff has performed together with opera greats like Maria Callas, although his off-stage relationship with fellow performers was often difficult.

Ghena Dimitrova

A soprano, Dimitrova´s voice is often described in superlatives. She was born in Beglej in 1941 and graduated from the Sofia Conservatory. In 1967, Dimitrova was catapulted to fame suddenly when the two primadonnas were unable to perform, and the young Ghena took on the role of Abigaille in Nabucco with aplomb. In 1970, she won a grant that led her to La Scala school. She has performed with the three tenors, Placido Domingo, Jose Carreras and Luciano Pavarotti. The opera world lost this golden voice in 2005.

Le Mystere des Voix Bulgares (The Mysterious Voices of Bulgaria) choir

The Mysterious Voices of Bulgaria, a recording by the National Radio And Television premier women's choir, popularised worldwide traditional Bulgarian music in the late 1980s. *Yanka Rupkina*, the musical leader from the choir, later also worked with Kate Bush and Chris de Burgh.

Valya Balkanska

Born in the Rhodope mountains in 1942, Balkanska imbibed from young all the traditional folk songs from her mother and grandmother. She has the honour of having her performance of *Izlel e Delyo Haidutin* included in the Voyager Golden Record sent off on board the Voyager spacecraft in 1977. The record is intended to give any extra-terrestrial being which comes across it an idea of what earthlings sound like.

Christo

Remember the husband and wife pair of artists who wrapped the Reichstag in Berlin in 1995, and erected 7,500 giant metal gates in New York´s Central Park in 2005? Christo (the husband) is Bulgarian. Their dramatic style of art has earned them both admiration and derision, but the pair remain unfazed by criticisms.

Sports Stars
Albena Denkova and Maxim Staviiski
The ice dance pair won won the World Championships in Calgary in 2006 and Tokyo in 2007.

Olympic Medallists
Bulgaria has a long list of Olympic champions and silver and bronze medallists. They include: Nikola Stanchev, Valentin Yordanov and Armen Nazaryan (wrestling), Stefka Kostadinova (high jump), Tereza Marinova (triple jump), Ekaterina Dafovska and Irina Nikulchina (biathlon) and Evgenia Radanova (speed skating).

Dimitar Berbatov
Currently with Tottenham Hotspurs, the Bulgarian striker started his football career with CSKA Sofia as an 18-year-old in the 1998-99 season. Named Bulgarian Player of the Year in 2002, 2004 and 2005, Berbatov has scored 31 goals in 50 senior international appearances and was also an impressive scorer for Bayer Leverkusen in the German Bundesliga. He has played Champions League football for Bayer Leverkusen including the final against Real Madrid in 2002 and was in the Bulgarian squad for the European Championships in Portugal in 2004.

Berbatov moved to Tottenham from Bayer Leverkusen for £10,6 M and proved an instant hit in the English Premier League. He has also won the Barclays Player of the Month award. Berbatov follows in the footsteps of other famous Bulgarian kickers before him, such as Stoichkov, Balukov, Mihailov and Lechkov in the 1990s.

Mahlyanov Kaloyan Stefanov (aka Kotooshu Katsunori)
Better known as Kotooshu Katsunori, he is a rikishi (a professional sumo wrestler). Stefanov was born in Veliko Tarnovo in 1983 and made his debut in Japan in November 2002. He amazed everyone with his meteoric rise to the rank of ozeki (second highest rank) in 2005, becoming the first European to achieve this rank.

At 204 cm (6 ft. 8 ins) and weighing 143 kg (315 pounds), Stefanov is considered lean by sumo standards.

Stefanov´s boyish good looks has earned him the moniker the `David Beckham of Sumo´, which he dislikes, and landed him the job as the face of Meiji Dairies Corporation´s Bulgarian yoghurt. He is dubbed by Japanese media as Bulgaria´s best known export after its yoghurt (which is a big hit with the Japanese).

Veselin Topalov

The April 2007 FIDE rating ranks Topalov second in the world with an Elo rating of 2772. Born in Rousse in 1975, he learnt to play chess at eight from his father, going on to win the Under 14 Championship in Puerto Rico (1989) and the silver medal at the World Under-16 Championship in Singapore (1990). He became a grandmaster in 1992, and at the chess Olympiad in 1994, he beat Gary Kasparov. He won the FIDE World Championship in 2005.

Antoaneta Stefanova

Stefanova was born in 1979 in Sofia. She was introduced to the game of chess at the tender age of four by her father. She won the 2004 Women´s World Championships.

Media
Ralitsa Vassileva

Sofia-born Vassileva is an anchor for CNN International, which she joined in 1992. Based at CNN's global headquarters in Atlanta, she anchors Your World Today and World News. She began her career at CNN as anchor of CNN World Report. Before joining CNN, Vassileva was a highly-rated anchor and reporter for Bulgarian Television (BT). Vassileva's interest in journalism began after she joined Bulgarian Radio's English language service in 1987 as an English translator and announcer.

Sensational Murder Victim
Georgi Markov

Famous in a horrific way (like Alexander Litvinenko, the Putin critic who died from radiation poisoning in London in 2006), Markov was a dissident who was murdered in London in 1978. The murder weapon was straight out of a Bond movie—an innocuous umbrella that fired a dart filled with the poison ricin.

PLACES OF INTEREST
The following is not an exhaustive list of the gems Bulgaria has to offer, but an appetiser of the country's treasures.

Alexander Nevski Memorial Church
Built to express gratitude to the Russians for liberating Bulgaria from Ottoman grip, the foundation stone was laid in 1882. This impressive piece of architecture is named after the patron saint of the Russian emperor, Alexander II. Occupying an area of about 3,170 sq m (34,121 sq ft), the church can accommodate 5,000 worshippers. The Orthodox church services (with the special Gregorian-chant like singing) is made exceptionally moving by the acoustics of the church.

Rila Monastery
Placed on the list of UNESCO´s World Cultural Heritage since 1983, the monastery is about 120 km (74.56 miles) from Sofia. Founded in the 10th century, a huge fire in 1833 devoured most of the monastery, leaving only Hrelyo´s Tower as the only surviving building from the 14th century. Apart from the beauty of the monastery itself, its location, set among the tranquil mountains, makes a visit to the monastery quite a magical experience.

Bachkovo Monastery
This is the second largest monastery in Bulgaria and is also on UNESCO´s list as a World Cultural Heritage. Founded in 1083 by two Georgian brothers, many of the the monastery´s murals and icons are painted by Bulgaria´s best known Revival Period artist, Zahari Zograf. Like Rila, its location makes it a good choice to escape the madding crowd.

The icon of the Virgin Mary from Bachkovo, Rila and Troyan monasteries are regarded as miracle-working. These

Attractions in Plovdiv include the ancient theatre that dates back to the second century.

were brought to Sofia's Alexander Nevski Church under tight security in May 2007 for special prayers for the release of the Bulgarian medics who were at that time still languishing in a Libyan prison for allegedly infecting children with the HIV virus. Miracle, coincidence, good negotiation skills of the EU or all three, the medics were indeed freed and returned to Bulgaria in July 2007.

Plovdiv

You will hear a lot about the National Revival Period (after Bulgaria threw off the yoke of Ottoman repression) when in Bulgaria. The old city of Plovdiv is the place to go to get an idea of the typical architecture of this period. Many of the houses along the cobble-stoned streets have been lovingly restored, thanks to Atanas Vasilev Krastev, one-time mayor of Plovdiv, who was responsible for the restoration of some 130 monuments. Most are now museums or restaurants. There is also a Roman theatre from the second century, discovered by fluke in 1972 because of a landslide. The city centre itself has a feel of old Europe and enough attractive shops for compulsive shoppers.

Veliko Tarnovo

The capital of the Second Bulgarian Kingdom (1185–1396) and the place where the first Bulgarian constitution was adopted. Veliko Tarnovo´s main attraction is the medieval citadel of Tsarevets.

Arbanasi

Just 4 km (2.5 miles) northeast of Veliko Tarnovo is the charming village of Arbanasi. This architectural and museum reserve is also a tourist favourite, showcasing the impressive stone houses of the wealthy Arbanasi, the beautifully decorated churches (especially the Church of the Nativity) and fountains.

Mount Vitosha

Only half an hour away by car from Sofia, Mt.Vitosha is the favourite weekend escape for Sofianites. Hiking and

These beautiful houses in Plovdiv are designed in the National Revival Period style.

СТАРИННА

picnicking in summer and skiing in winter, Mt.Vitosha is a popular destination all year round.

Trigrad Gorge and Environs

Bulgaria´s Grand Canyon, this gorge is found in the Rhodope mountains. The Trigrad river gets swallowed up by the appropriately named Devil´s Throat (*Dyavolsko Gurlo*), a cave with a huge black abyss. In the nearby gorge of the Boynovska River is the longest cave in the Rhodopes, the Yagodinska Cave (7.5 km/4.66 miles).

Belogradchik Rock Formations

The amazing work of art of Nature is found in the western foothills of the Balkan mountains. The reddish rock formations extend over an area of about 30 km (18.64 miles) long and 3 km (1.86 miles) wide. One of Bulgaria´s best preserved fortresses is also found here.

Black Sea Coast

Bulgaria´s entire eastern border is the Black Sea coast. Such an expansive coast naturally offers not only stretches of sandy beaches, but also fishing villages, Byzantine churches (such as in Nessebur), fortresses, birdwatching and (again!) fascinating rock formations, 17 km (10.56 miles) west of Varna.

CULTURE QUIZ

SITUATION 1

You are touring the countryside when you suddenly see an old man playing what looks like a bagpipe to you. Knowing that your family in Scotland will be fascinated to know Bulgarians also have bagpipes, you go up to the man pointing at your camera to ask if you can take his picture. He shakes his head vigorously. Should you:

🅐 Walk away disappointed that the Bulgarians are so unfriendly

🅑 Take out a 2 leva note and try to cajole the man to let you take his picture

🅒 Go ahead and snap anyway; you don´t know when you´ll come across a bagpipe again

Comments

🅒 is the option to take, not because you should ignore the man´s wishes, but because he has actually given you permission to do so. In Bulgaria, a nod means `no´ and a shake of the head means `yes´.

SITUATION 2

It´s your first New Year´s Eve in Sofia. You´ve heard about the celebrations in the city centre square and make your way there just before midnight. At midnight, fireworks go off, and everyone joins in a Horo dance and so do you. When you stop to gasp for air, you feel something poking your back. You swing round and see a young child grinning from ear to ear, holding a twig which he had apparently scratched you with. You should react by:

🅐 Snatching the twig from him and snap it into two in anger at his impudence

🅑 Grabbing the twig and thrusting it at him a few times, yelling `On guard!´

🅒 Grinning and giving him a `high five´. Heck, boys will be boys!

D Decide to go home straightaway before you´re attacked by mad children again

Comments
C is the closest to the right answer although instead of a `high five´, give him a lev. It´s a tradition on New Year´s Day for young children go around with a twig from the cornel tree, often decorated with dried fruits, popcorn and ring-shaped buns (*sourvaknitsa*), tapping people on the back to bring them prosperity and health. Although this is traditionally done to family members, children in the cities may tap strangers in the hope of getting a token in return.

SITUATION 3
Your colleague invites you to his home for dinner. You know from the photos proudly displayed on his desk that he has two kids, around 5 and 8. You have also learnt that it´s good manners to bring gifts, so you arm yourself with flowers (odd number of stems!), a bottle of whisky and a little box of chocolates. When your colleague opens the front door, you almost stumble across a few pairs of shoes. You should:

A Cheerfully say to your colleague, `Yo, Plamen, shoe rack not ready yet?´
B Pretend you didn´t notice the mess and walk right in
C Make a mental note to bring a shoe rack as a practical gift the next time you´re invited.

Comments
Any of the above would be commiting a faux pas. Bulgarians do have a habit of removing outdoor shoes before entering a home. You should always ask if you should remove your shoes before entering a home. Make a note to put on a pair of socks without holes when you´re visiting a Bulgarian home!

SITUATION 4
There´s a long queue at the airport check-in. Already feeling irritated, having woken up at 5:00 am to catch this early flight, you are just about to put your luggage onto the conveyor belt

when an Exterminator-looking type with gold chains shoves past you and jumps your queue. Do you:

Ⓐ Tap him on the shoulders and say firmly `Excuse me, I was here before you´.
Ⓑ Say `om´ and breathe deeply
Ⓒ Shove back and put your luggage with a bang onto the belt
Ⓓ Rely on sarcasm. Say loudly, `My goodness, and I thought Bulgaria was in the EU!´

Comments
If you value your life, don´t do **Ⓐ**, **Ⓒ** or **Ⓓ**, although with **Ⓓ** you may survive if the Exterminator doesn´t understand English. The chap is probably one of those mutri fellows (the Bulgarian underworld). They are prone to pumping their underworld rivals with bullets, and are usually armed. There´s no saying what he might do if you annoy him.

SITUATION 5
You have been emailing, faxing and discussing for many hours with a potential business contact. You like the sound of the Bulgarian CEO you´ve been talking to and if you allow yourself a little immodesty, the CEO seems to like your proposals and you too. It´s decided that you should fly to Sofia to close the deal. You arrive for the meeting with the CEO, and after all the warm handshakes and exchange of business cards and brochures, you take out the draft contract and prepare to run through the terms with him. The CEO starts to ask you if this is the first time you´re in Bulgaria, how long you intend to stay, if you like wine, if you have children and other seemingly irrelevant questions. How should you get him to focus on the business on hand?

Ⓐ Toy with the draft contract conspicuously to signal you want to talk business
Ⓑ Answer his question about your length of stay in Bulgaria loudly `One day´.
Ⓒ Keep looking at your watch pointedly, and say `I don´t like

to talk about my private life´.

D Remain affable and ask him a few `irrelevant´ questions too

Comments

A **B** and **C** are obviously too brusque, even rude. Bulgarians need a longer time than the average American or Briton to `get to the point´. The `irrelevant´ chatter is their way to size you up and is very relevant to all business dealings. Time is needed to build a relationship, but once that is achieved, you´ll find the Bulgarians rather straightforward business people. If it´s your first time meeting a Bulgarian contact, plan at least a week´s stay, and if you can, read up a bit about Bulgarian wine for chatting purposes. Some knowledge of Bulgarian wine or the history of Cyrillic will endear you to your business partners.

SITUATION 6

You are driving with your colleague to Rousse (close to the border with Romania). You notice the potholes on the road and ask your colleague, half in jest, why Bulgarian roads are so bad. His reply is that Bulgaria spent 500 years under the Turks. You should:

A Laugh and say `come on, that was more than 100 years ago!´

B Argue with him for the rest of the journey on why his answer is irrational

C Tell him in soothing tones that it´s time to let go, and forgive and forget

Comments

The above answers are all tosh, as in the first place, it´s insensitive to make such a remark to a Bulgarian, although someone actually did. Bulgarians are only too aware of the problems in their country and that the country´s image is fairly dented with many. That the Bulgarians suffered under the Ottoman Turks is beyond question, and this still pains present-day Bulgarians, hence the Ottoman yoke is a convenient whipping boy. Coupled with that, the uprisings against the Ottoman Turks and the revolutionaries who led them are always invoked by politicians when drumming up national pride, hence Bulgarians have this fixation about the Ottoman Turks. It´s not for foreigners to decide who their bete noire should be.

SITUATION 7

A Bulgarian asks you if you can speak Bulgarian or if you´re studying the language. You respond:

ⓐ Never! Cyrillic is so terribly difficult. Why don´t you all adopt the Latin alphabet?

ⓑ Admit you´re struggling, but you´re trying your best

ⓒ Gush about the beauty of the language and how fascinating you find it

ⓓ Why did you all have to take the Russian alphabet? Latin is so much easier.

Comments

Learning the Cyrillic alphabet and the Bulgarian language is a challenge for most foreigners. Whatever frustrations you may feel about the difficulty, remember that Bulgarians are immensely proud of having founded Cyrillic. It´s therefore an awful crime to criticise the alphabet/language in any way, and it´s definitely death knell for you to think that they took the language from the Russians! Learn at your own pace, or even not at all, but never say anything negative about Cyrillic/Bulgarian, although you don´t have to exaggerate your appreciation.

SITUATION 8

You´ve lost count of the number of trips you´ve made to the residency permit office on Maria Luisa Boulevard. On previous occasions, there was always some other document they needed each time you went there. Last week, you asked the officer to list down exactly the documents needed, as you want to get to get it right once and for all. You go with all the documents, hand them in and the lady at the counter says that your marriage certificate must be legalised by your embassy in Russia (as your country doesn´t have a diplomatic representation in Bulgaria and the one in Russia is the nearest). What should you do?

Ⓐ Quietly go home and figure out how you can arrange for that to be done
Ⓑ Take out 40 leva and slip it to her under the stack of (rejected) documents
Ⓒ Scream at her and demand to see her boss

Comments

Understand that in many emerging countries, salaries for public servants are so laughable that they have to make ends meet by trying to squeeze bribes from people beholden to them. Losing your temper can only make things worse. It´s unpleasant and it may be against your principles to bribe, but you are at their mercy. **Ⓐ** is the best option, in this case. Go home but it doesn´t mean you really have to do as you´re told. Although it costs a bit more, you can appoint a lawyer to take care of the entire process for you. The advantage is that they speak the language and know the ins and outs of the bureaucracy, preventing you from bursting a blood vessel.

If you´re lucky enough to know somebody in a position of power, asking the person for help usually gets things moving very quickly. Of course, you may be called upon to return the favour some day, so you have decide if it´s worth it.

DO'S AND DON'TS

DO'S

- Practise shaking your head when saying *da* (yes) and nodding your head when saying *ne* (no).
- Learn some Bulgarian and at least the Cyrillic alphabet. It´s easier to get around.
- Find out about Bulgarian wine and food and the history of Cyrillic. Bulgarians will be delighted when you show an interest in the things they´re immensely proud of.
- Be aware that Bulgarians still feel pain about the 500 years under the Ottoman Turks.
- Get to know who Vassil Levski was and what phrases like `April Uprising´ and `Batak massacre´ refer to.
- Have heaps of patience; it´s not worth shortening your life getting mad at the bureaucracy or lack of punctuality.
- Try *boza* at least once.
- Be modestly dressed when visiting places of worship.
- Enjoy what Bulgaria has to offer (e.g.beauty of nature)

DON´TS

- Fight with anyone, even if you think you're right; it might be a *mutri* (underworld type) and they´re always right and armed.
- Say Cyrillic came from the Russians!
- Openly display your homosexuality. It´s not quite accepted by the majority of Bulgarians.
- Openly display your wealth, unless you want to lose lots of it fast.
- Cringe visibly when you see a Bulgarian eating chicken hearts. Just pretend it´s chocolate hearts.
- Trust the `green man´ at traffic lights. Always check for colour- blind drivers driving through red lights .
- Buy a flashy car or leave your car in a quiet street. It may disappear very soon.
- Push your business partner to `make up his mind´, before he´s had time to build a relationship with you.
- Try to replicate 100 per cent your lifestyle at home here. Have a go at something different.

GLOSSARY

STARTER KIT OF WORDS AND PHRASES

English	Bulgarian
Good Morning	*Dobro utro*
Good Day	*Dobur den*
Good Evening	*Dobur vecher*
Good Night	*Leka nosht*
Goodbye	*Dovizhdane / (informal) Chow, like Italian Ciao*
Yes	*Da (shake your head!)*
No	*Ne (nod!)*
Maybe	*Mozhe bi*
Do you speak English?	*Govorite li angliiski?*
I don´t understand	*Ne razbiram*
I don´t speak Bulgarian	*Az ne govorya berlgarski*
Excuse me	*Izvinete*
Sorry	*Proshtavaite*
No problem	*Nyamo problame*
Thank you	*Blagodarya / (informal) mersi, like French merci*
Not at all	*Nyamo Zashto*
(to the) Left	*Na Lyavo*
(to the) Right	*Na Dyasno*
Straight (on)	*Na pravo*
Here	*Tuk*
There	*Tam*
Now	*Sega*
Today	*Dness*
Tomorrow	*Utre*

English	Bulgarian
How much? (asking for price)	*Kolko struva?*

COMMON TERMS

English	Bulgarian
Public bath or spa	*Banya or Bani*
City or town	*Grad*
Garden	*Gradina*
Monastery	*Manastir*
Market	*Pazar*
Mountain	*Planina*
Town Square	*Ploshtad*
Saint	*Sveti/(f) Sveta*
Street	*Ulitsa*

NUMBERS

English	Bulgarian
0	*Nula*
1	*Edin/Edna/Edno*
2	*Dve/dwa*
3	*Tri*
4	*Chetiri*
5	*Pet*
6	*Shest*
7	*Sedem*
8	*Osem*
9	*Devet*
10	*Deset*
11	*Edinadeset/edinayset*
12	*Dvanadeset/dvanayset*
13	*Trinadeset/Trinayset*

English	Bulgarian
14	*Chetirinadeset/Chetirinayset*
15	*Petnadeset/Petnayset*
16	*Shestnadeset/Shestnayset*
17	*Sedemnadeset/Sedemnayset*
18	*Osemnadeset/Osemnayset*
19	*Devetnadeset/Devetnayset*
20	*Dvadeset/Dvayset*
30	*Trideset/triyset*
40	*Chetirideset/chetiriyset*
50	*Petdeset*
60	*Shestdeset/Sheyset*
70	*Sedemdeset*
80	*Osemdeset*
90	*Devetdeset*
100	*Sto*
500	*Petstotin*
1000	*Hilyada*
1 million	*Edin milion*
1 billion	*Edin miliard*

VITAL SIGNS

English	Bulgarian
Entrance	ВХОД
Exit	ИЗХОД
No entry!	ВХОД ЗАБРАНЕН!
Ladies´ (lavatory)	ЖЕНИ / ДАМИ
Men´s (lavatory)	МЪЖЕ
Caution!	ВНИМАНИЕ!

RESOURCE GUIDE

EMERGENCY NUMBERS
- Ambulance: 150
- Police: 166
- Fire: 160
- Traffic police: 982-2723

NB: The person at the other end of the line may not always be able to speak English.

Area Codes for Telephone Numbers
- Country code : 359

Main City Codes, add 0 in front if dialing from within Bulgaria.

Blagoevgrad	73	Bourgas	56
Dobrich	58	Gabrovo	66
Haskovo	38	Kardjali	361
Kyustendil	78	Lovech	68
Montana	96	Pazardjik	34
Pernik	76	Pleven	64
Plovdiv	32	Razgrad	84
Rousse	82	Shumen	54
Silistra	86	Sliven	44
Smolyan	301	SOFIA	2
Stara Zagora	42	Targovishte	601
Varna	52	Veliko Tarnovo	62
Vidin	94	Vratsa	92
Yambol	46		

When dialing from inside Bulgaria:
- Add `0´ in front of city code
- When calling a fixed line number from a mobile phone, add `0´ + city code in front of number even if you´re calling from within the same city
- International dial-out code: 00

USEFUL WEBSITES
Government website
- http://www.government.bg
  Has links to the other government ministries.

Map and Guide
- http://www.map-guide.bg
  This site has a comprehensive list of maps for all over Bulgaria. Additionally, there are listings of hotels, restaurants, car rental companies, airlines, courier companies and useful information about Bulgaria.

Expatriate Information
- http://www.expatinbulgaria.com
- http://www.britishexpat.com/Bulgaria.802.0.html

Country/City Information
- http://www.visittobulgaria.com
- http://www.sofiacityguide.com
- http://www.plovdivcityguide.com
- http://www.selo.bg
  This site focuses on the countryside of Bulgaria. It gives you a great virtual tour from the comfort of home (or office, if you´re using corporate time!)

Events, Restaurants, Cinemas etc
- http://www.programata.bg
  This website lets you search for information on classical music, concerts, movies, restaurants, videos and DVDs, club music and more in a city of your choice : Sofia, Plovdiv, Varna, Bourgas and Stara Zagora.

Business and Economics
- http://www.investbg.government.bg
- American Chamber of Commerce
  http://www.amcham.bg
- British Bulgarian Chamber of Commerce
  http://www.bbcc.bg

- Bulgarian Chamber of Commerce and Industry
  http://www.bcci.bg
- Bulgarian Dutch Business Club
  http://www.bg-nl.com
- German-Bulgarian Chamber of Industry and Commerce
  http://www.bulgarien.ahk.de
- Italian Chamber of Commerce
  http://www.camcomit.bg

Business facilities in Sofia
- Business Park Sofia.
  htp://www.businesspark-sofia.com
- Executive Centre.
  http://www.executivecentre.com/service-office-locations/
  the-executive-centre-sofia-saborna.html
- Inter Expo Centre
  http://www.bulgarreklama.com

DIPLOMATIC MISSIONS
- **Australia** 37, Trakia St. Tel: 946 1334
- **Canada** 9, Moskovska St. Tel: 969 9710
- **India** 23, Sveti Sedmochislenitsi St. Tel: 963 5675
- **South Africa** 26, Bacho Kiro St. Tel: 989 5015
- **United Kingdom** 9, Moskovska St, Tel: 933 9222
- **United States of America** 16, Kozyak St. Tel: 937 5100

For other diplomatic missions, see:
- http://www.bcci.bg/services/info/embassy.htm
- *Sofia in your pocket*
- *Sofia the Insider´s Guide*

TOURIST INFORMATION
National Tourist Information Centre
Ploshtad Sveta Nedelya 1, 1040 Sofia
Tel: 933 5811 / 933 5845
www.bulgariatravel.org

HOSPITALS
Sofia
- Pirogov
  21, Totleben Blvd. Tel: 915 4411
  This is Sofia´s main hospital where all emergency cases
  are brought
- Lozenetz Hospital
  1 Kozyak St. Tel: 960 7681
- Tokuda Hospital Sofia
  51B, Nikola Vaptsarov Blvd
  Tel: 403 4000
- Vita Medical Centre & Hospital
  9, Dragovitsa St. Tel: 943 4398 / 960 4950

Plovdiv
- 1st City Hospital
  59, Ivan Vassil Street. Tel: 224 306 / 07 / 08

Varna
- City Hospital
  40, Saborna Blvd. Tel: 223 041

- A list of hospitals and medical centres is available from
  American Embassy´s US Citizens´ Service. http://sofia.
  usembassy.gov/hospitals4.html
- Another site with hospital listings is http://www.need.bg/
  en/?c = 77

VETERINARIANS
- Blue Cross Veterinary Clinic
  1, Chereshova Gradina St, Pantcharevo, Sofia
  Tel: 979 0935 (Emergencies) 089 836 1903
  http://www.bluecrossbg.com
  They also have a pet hotel.
- Dr. Antov Veterinary Clinic
  4, Plackovitsa St, Lorenetz, Sofia. Tel: 089 883 1283
- Another site with a listing of veterinary clinics is
  http://www.need.bg/en/?c = 139&page = 0

NEWSPAPERS AND MAGAZINES
Print Media
The Sofia Echo
Established in 1997, this is the only English-language newspaper. This weekly is an excellent source of news and other useful information such as listings of what's on, TV programmes and restaurant reviews. Its website, http://www.sofiaecho.com has useful links to other sources of information, including the foreign community portal at http://www.expatinbulgaria.com. You can also sign up for the free daily news bulletin, which gives you a selection of the important news. As at January 2010, the subscription rates for the newspaper are 54 leva for 6 months and 90 leva for a year.

Vagabond
A monthly magazine carrying articles which provide readers with interesting information about the country. Articles cover different themes: political, economic, social and cultural. The Info Guide at the back of the magazine has useful tips for foreigners in Bulgaria, as well as restaurant reviews. This worthy magazine sets you back by only 4.99 leva.

The magazine is available from most magazine stands and hotel souvenir shops (but not Hilton and Sheraton Hotels in Sofia). To get an idea of the contents, go to http://www.vagabond-bg.com

Bulgarisches Wirtschaftsblatt und Südosteuropäischer Report
This is a monthly German-language newspaper with a focus on business in Bulgaria and South Eastern Europe. As at 2007, it costs 150 leva for a year's subscription.

Online Media
There are lots of English language news websites:
- http://www.bnr.bg
  You can get news and cultural tid-bits from this site, not only in English, but also in French, German, Turkish, Arabic and a host of other languages.

- http://www.novinite.com
  This site has selected free news articles, and a paid daily online newspaper, *Sofia Morning News*, covering the latest economic, political, cultural and sports news in Bulgaria, major world events and foreign media analyses. It costs 50 Euros for a year.
- http://www.standartnews.com/en
  This site also has news for free. The articles are concise, but they give you a general idea of what's going on.
- http://www.focus-fen.net
  This site of Focus Agency has up-to-date information (practically breaking news) of Bulgaria, Southeastern Europe, the Balkans and the world. Very practical summary of daily news for those who need a quick overview, and interviews and analyses for others wanting a bit more to chew on.
- http://news.dnevnik.bg
  The English site has news on mainly Bulgaria.

International newspapers like *International Herald Tribune, Financial Times, Economist, Time* and *Newsweek* are available at hotel and shopping mall newsstands. Magazines like *National Geographic, People, Hello!, OK!* and *Cosmopolitan* are also available. English language teachers who like using *Business Spotlight* for Business English classes will be able to lay their hands on this magazine (Bulgarian /English) as well.

ORGANISATIONS TO HELP YOU SETTLE IN

- International Women's Association of Sofia
  This non-profit organisation is a useful place to start for women (especially accompanying spouses) looking to network with and find out more about Bulgaria from other expatriates in Sofia. Membership is open to all women who are holders of foreign passports. The IWC's activities include a bridge group, patchwork-handicraft group, charity work group, a Book Club, tennis group, a Scrap Book Club, a German conversation group, an English conversation group; a Bulgarian crash conversation group, Newcomers' Coffee Mornings, bowling group, and Latino dancing.

Sorry, guys, there are usually more female accompanying partners than male, so networks are always orientated towards women. You can read more about the IWC at http://www.iwc-sofia.com

- Ecologic Consultancy Ltd (ECL)
  ECL provides Orientation and Adaptation courses and Thematic courses (such as Bulgarian Cuisine and Bond with Nature) to help bridge the cultural gap. The areas of study include cultural characteristics, values and beliefs, business etiquette and routines of daily life. The staff are all Bulgarians. The courses are conducted in English, although some of the staff members speak an additional language like Russian or German. The courses include field trips. More information can be found on their website at http://www.crossculturebg.com

EDUCATIONAL INSTITUTIONS
Most of the educational institutions with an international student body are in Sofia. Outside the capital, you will have to depend on the local schools. Many of the local schools do have classes in English, German or French, but they follow a Bulgarian curriculum and proficiency in Bulgarian is needed.

English Language
- International Children's Creativity Foundation
  This English-speaking kindergarten for tots aged 2 to 6 is popular with the international community. They offer morning and full-day programmes. Located at, 36 Vaklinets St, Dragalevtsi-Simeonovo. Sofia (near supermarket MAXI). Tel: (+359-2) 967 3112
- *Wonder World*
  An all-day kindergarten, it caters to three age groups: 2-3 years; 3-5 years, and 5-7 years. Classes are in English and Bulgarian. They also offer (oft–lauded) babysitting services. Hours: 8:30am—3:00pm. They are at located at 2A Matochina Street, Dragalevtsi
  Tel: (+359-2) 967 2099
  Email: wonder_world@vip.orbitel.bg.

- The Anglo-American School
  The school moved into their brand new, purpose-built campus located at the foot of the Vitosha mountains in September 2006. In 2007, the school had 215 students of 35 nationalities, from kindergarten to 12th grade. The curriculum offered is a combination of both US and UK best practice. A list of department-specific emails can be found on their website.
  Website: http://www.aas-sofia.org
  Tel: (+359-2) 923 8810
- American English Academy
  This school offers classes from kindergarten to secondary (up to grade 12). The school is at 4th Flr, 150 School, Deliyska Vodenitsa, Druzhba 2, Sofia 1582.
  Website: http://www.aea-bg.com
  Tel: (+359-2) 973 1222 / 886 850 255
  Email: aeaoffice@gmail.com
- The American College of Sofia
  The campus is in Mladost and offers an American curriculum to Bulgarian and International students from Grade 9 through Grade 12.
  Website: http://www.acs.bg
  Tel: (+359-2) 434 1008 / 434 1010 / 434 1011
  Email: acs@acs.bg
- The American University in Bulgaria
  The main campus is located in Blagoevgrad, a city about 100 km south of Sofia, and offers an American-style liberal arts education. Its executive MBA programme and Centre for European Programmes are offered at the Elieff Center for Education and Culture, Studentski Grad, Sofia. A list of department-specific emails can be found on their website.
  Website: http://www.aubg.bg
  Tel: Blagoevgrad: (+359-73) 888 235
  Sofia: (+359-2) 960 7940 / 960 7942

German Language
Deutsche Schule Erich Kastner
This is located at 6 Lyulin, Sofia.
Website: http//:www.kestnerschool.com
Tel: (+359-2) 824 459 / 826 7280

French Language
Le Lycée Victor Hugo
110 Simeonovsko Chaussée quarter Vitosha
Website:http://www.vhugo.org
Tel: (+359-2) 963 2119 / 963 2964 / 866 0105

CULTURAL CENTRES
- British Council
  7, Krakra St, Sofia. Tel: 942 4344
- French Cultural Institute
  2, Dyakon Ignati St. Sofia. Tel: 937 7922
- Goethe Institute
  1, Budapesta St. Sofia. Tel: 939 0100
- The Cervantes Institute
  1, Saborna St. Sofia. Tel: 810 4500

TELECOMMUNICATIONS COMPANIES
- Bulgarian Telecommunications Company
  http://www.btc.bg/en
- Orbitel
  http://www.orbitel.bg/en
- Spectrum Net
  http://www.spnet.net
- Cable Tel
  http://www.cabletel.bg

MOBILE PHONE COMPANIES
- Globul
  http://www.globul.bg
- Mtel
  http://www.mtel.bg
- Vivatel (owned by Bulgarian Telecommunications Co)
  http://www.vivatel.bg

DIY SHOPS

- Praktiker
  323, Tsarigradsko Shosse, Sofia
  20, Obelsko Shosse, Sofia
  115A, Bulgaria Blvd, Plovdiv
  55, Republika Blvd, Varna

This German DIY chain has such an incredible range of DIY equipment, it will even get non-DIY types interested. They also have lightings, garden furniture and decor items. Their website is http://www.praktiker.bg

- Mr Bricolage
  171, Europe Blvd. Sofia

There are also stores in Plovdiv and Bourgas. This French competitor also carries a wide range of DIY tools.

PLACES OF WORSHIP

Although there are places of worship for different religions and denominations, obviously there is the question of the language to consider. Below are a few churches in Sofia which have services in English.

- The Anglican Church
  A meeting is held every third Sunday at the British ambassador´s residence. For more details, contact the British embassy in Sofia.

- International Baptist Church Sofia
  Services are in English, held every Sunday at the World Trade Center (Interpred) with Adult Bible Study at 10am and worship at 11am. Their website is http://www. IBCSworld.org

- The Bulgarian Lutheran Church
  Services in English are held at 9am on Sundays at 4, Kapitan Andreev St (Lozenets). Their website is http://www. celc.info/?bulgaria01.php

DIRECTORIES

The directory business is fairly young: *Yellow Pages* and *Golden Pages* are currently in the market. *Golden Pages* directory started distribution of the Sofia directory in May 2007. *Golden Pages* for other cities started end of 2007.

- http://www.yellowpages-bg.com
- http://www.goldenpages.bg

BOOKSHOPS

There are a number of bookshops in Sofia which carry a wide range of English (and other European languages) books:

- Booktrading
  15 Graf Ignatiev St.
  Two floors with a wide range of novels, English classics, hobby books, travel books (lots of interesting books about Bulgaria), maps, children´s books, phrase books, dictionaries, greeting cards, gift bags and postcards
- Orange
  18, Graf Ignatiev St
  It appears deceptively as if it´s next door to Booktrading, but it isn´t. Turn right as you come out of Booktrading and walk about 300 metres, past the traffic light junction
  This place has five storeys; a restaurant is on the fifth floor and books (from Knigomania chain) on the fourth. Apart from the usual suspects, I even saw a book on English jurispridence here, among the many finance and accounting books! There are also SAT, and TOEFL preparation books and an exercise book for 100 Chinese characters. Third floor houses CDs and the like, second floor is the kids´ territory, and ground floor (or American first floor) is a gift shop (expensive pens, pen holders etc). You can get your stationery in the basement, as well as print your own T-shirt.
- Knigomania
  Top floor, Mall of Sofia
  101, Alexander Stamboliiski St.
  Huge store full of paperbacks, guidebooks, CDs and DVDs. Browser friendly and family-friendly in that family members who are not bookworms can go shopping, watch

a movie (IMAX next door), or drink a coffee elsewhere in the mall.

Knigomania is also at 28, Vassil Levski Blvd and 17, Praga Blvd.

SUPERMARKETS
- Piccadilly
  City Centre Sofia. 2, Arsenalski Blvd., Sofia
  Mall of Sofia. 101, Alexander Stamboliiski Blvd, Sofia
  Outlets also in Varna, Bourgas, Veliko Tarnovo and Plovdiv
- Hit
  Alexander Malinov Blvd, Mladost 4, Sofia
- Kaufland
  Philip Avramov Blvd, Maldost 3, Sofia
- Billa
  Many outlets in Sofia (e.g. near HIT) and in the other cities, Look out for an enormous yellow and red shopping bag shape twirling in the air; it´s Billa´s signpost)
- Familia
  Chain of smaller stores with many outlets in Sofia (one along Arsenalski Blvd, about 200 m from City Centre Sofia)
- Fantastiko
  28 outlets in Sofia plus an outlet in Kyustendil (opened in October 2007).
- Elemag
  4, Zlatovruh St , Sofia
  19, Koziak St, Sofia (near American Embassy)
  30, Elemag St, Sofia

OPEN MARKETS
The open markets in Sofia are at:
- Stefan Stambolov Blvd (the famous Zhenski Pazar)
- Shipchenski Prohod Blvd (near Romanian embassy)
- Graf Ignatiev Street
- Hristo Smirnenski Blvd (opposite Architecture School)
- At the end of Kraishte street (off Vitosha Boulevard near Yuzhen Park. Follow the tram lines. It´s just beyond the tiny post office on your right).

PHARMACIES
In the main cities, you will find many well-stocked pharmacies. Just look for the sign
` А П Т Е К А ´ (pronounced Apteka).

INTERNATIONAL RADIO STATIONS
- Deutsche Welle   95.7 MHz FM
- Radio France Int´l   103.6 MHz FM

LANGUAGE COURSES
- The Department of Language Learning, Sofia University St. Kliment Ohridski
  http://www.deo.uni-sofia.bg
- Alexander Language Schools Franchise
  http://www.als-alexander.org
- Mastylo language School, Plovdiv
  http://www.mastylo.net

AIRLINES
- Air France
  9, Fritjof Nansen St. Tel: 939 7010, 939 7050
  http://www.airfrance.com/bg
- Alitalia
  5, Angel Kunchev St. Tel: 980 2212 / 980 0864
- Austrian Airlines
  41, Vitosha Blvd. Tel: 980 2323, 981 2424
  http://www.aua.com/bg/bul
- British Airways
  49, Patriarch Evtimii Blvd. Tel: 954 7000, 945 9227
  http://www.britishairways.com
- Bulgaria Air
  1, Brussels Blvd. Tel: 937 3254
  E-mail: office@air.bg
  The website: htttp://www.air.bg also has contact numbers for ticketing enquiries in airports in other cities
- Hemus Air
  1 Brussels Blvd.
  Sales Office:
  Airport Sofia. Tel.: + 359-2 9420 213

Airport Varna. Tel./Fax: + 359 52 501 039
http://www.hemusair.bg
- Lufthansa German Airlines
  26-30 Bacho Kiro St.,
  Reservations: Tel: 930 4242
- Olympic Airlines
  55, Stamboliiski Blvd. Tel: 980 1040, 981 4545

For the cost conscious, take a look at the sites listed below or
or go directly to the websites of the low-cost carriers:
- http://www.expedia.com
- http://www.attitudetravel.com
- http://www.whichbudget.com

- Cimber Sterling
  http://www.cimber.com
- Germanwings
  http://www.germanwings.com
- Norwegian Air Shuttle
  http://www.norwegian.no
- SkyEurope
  http://www.skyeurope.com
- Wizz Air
  http://www.wizzair.com

FURTHER READING

GETTING TO KNOW BULGARIA

Sofia: The Insider's Guide

- This free quarterly guide is compact but very informative, which can be found in hotels, restaurants, places of entertainment and of culture in Sofia. In spite of its title, it is more than just about Sofia; the guide carries information about the country´s history, the people, language, sights, cuisine and other useful information for foreigners.

    Written by two foreigners married to Bulgarians, the information is honest and with an understanding of what foreigners usually want to know about their host country. Both authors have lived in Bulgaria for more than 10 years.

The Insider's guide to Sofia and beyond. Christine Milner and Paromita Sanatani. Sofia: Inside & Out Ltd, 2005

- The guide was so well- received by foreigners that the two authors, Christine Milner and Paromita Sanatani, went on to publish a book, the Insider´s Guide to Sofia and Beyond in 2005. This book is a more comprehensive version of the Guide; it has lots of useful information and beautiful pictures. Priced at BGN 24 (Euro 12.90), it is really a worthwhile investment. Readers particularly appreciate the frank insight the authors provide about their adopted country. Available in bookshops, souvenir shops and selected cultural centres. For more information, check out www.insidesofia.com

Sofia inyourpocket

- This is another very useful free guide, which comes out once every two months. Available from most hotels, this guide hands out valuable information with such an acute sense of humour that it´s worth reading the guide just for amusement alone. The guide also has a listing of cultural events, accommodation, restaurants, cinemas, art galleries, theatres and sports options. Alas, it´s basically for people based in Sofia.Go to http://www.inyourpocket.com for a sample of this pocket-sized gem

TRAVEL AND ACCOMMODATION
The Rough Guide to Bulgaria. Jonathan Bousfield and Dan Richardson. Rough Guides. 2005
- This book is particularly useful for those who prefer pottering around on your own, instead of following, sheep-like, the coloured umbrella of a tour guide. It has lots of interesting historical and cultural details, apart from practical recommendations for accommodation covering all budgets and useful city maps.

Bulgaria, Tour Guide. Kapka Nikolova, Dr. Georgi Vladimirov, Peter Moutafov, Yanka Kroumova. Sofia: Tangra TanNakRa, 2006.
- A detailed book about the many interesting sites in Bulgaria, with over 1,500 photos. If you don´t mind the sometimes gushing tone, the text and photos takes you to all corners of Bulgaria without your having to leave your couch.

HISTORY
The Rose of the Balkans: a Short History of Bulgaria. Ivan Ilchev. Colibri, 2005.
- The author is professor of modern History at the Sofia University, and was Visiting Professor at Chiba University, Japan and at the W. Wilson Center at the Smithsonian Institution in Washington, D.C. This book deals with the turbulent and complicated history of Bulgaria in an easy-to-absorb manner. A fair account is given without too many superlatives, a common tendency with local authors.

A Short History of Modern Bulgaria. R.J.Crampton. Cambridge Universtiy Press, Second Edition, 2005
- Various sources recommend this book for an informative and readable account of Bulgaria´s history.

BUSINESS
The Report: Emerging Bulgaria 2007 published by Oxford Business Group, a UK publishing and consulting group, provides business and economic analysis. Part of a series of annual reports, the report is compiled by a team of

analysts sent to Bulgaria for six months to interview some 300 individuals (government officials and private sector executives). A weekly online economic briefing is also available to subscribers. http://www.oxfordbusinessgroup. com has more details

PROPERTY
Propertywise
- `The magazine for property investors in Bulgaria´, as the magazine describes itself. For 6 leva, the magazine provides reliable and honest opinions about the property market. Even those not looking for property will find the articles informative.

Quest Bulgaria
- Another useful source (see http://www.questbulgaria.com)

Buying a Property in Bulgaria. Jonathan White. How To Books Ltd, 2005.
- Practical advice on buying property written with a sense of humour.

LITERATURE
For those who are able to read German, the following two books give readers an insight into Bulgaria of earlier years and Bulgarians themselves. The author is a German-Jew, who fled Nazi-Germany with her Jewish mother to Bulgaria in 1939. She returned to Germany in 1947, and as an adult, she lived in Paris, Germany and Israel, making nostalgic trips back to Bulgaria.

Die Reise Nach Sofia. Angelika Schrobsdorff. Deutscher Taschenbuch Verlag GmbH & Co. KG, 16th edition 2003

Grandhotel Bulgaria. Heimkehr in die Vergangenheit. Angelika Schrobsdorff. Deutscher Taschenbuch Verlag GmbH & Co. KG, 2nd Edition, 2003

ABOUT THE AUTHOR

Agnes Sachsenroeder first cut her teeth crossing cultures in Egypt in 1997. After more than a decade of being a desk-bound legal adviser, she morphed into a travelling, trailing spouse as her husband´s posting took them to Cairo that year. Wet behind the ears as a first time expatriate wife, she had to battle all the classic symptoms of culture shock, until she learned that her funny moods could be attributed to this disease which liked to attack expatriates. Once she found her expatriate bearings, Sachsenroeder joined a volunteer organisation in Cairo as coordinator of a newcomers´ orientation programme, which focused on helping newcomers adjust to a new environment.

After six years in Cairo, she was to cross cultures again when they moved to Berlin. Two years later, she trailed her husband to his next posting in Bucharest, Romania. Just when she thought she had started to settle in, someone decided that she should be exposed to yet another culture, and they moved to Sofia, Bulgaria.

Culture Shock! Bulgaria is the author´s swan song of sorts. Her tour of duty as a trailing spouse ended in 2008.

INDEX

Titles in the CultureShock! series:

Argentina	France	Portugal
Australia	Germany	Russia
Austria	Great Britain	San Francisco
Bahrain	Hawaii	Saudi Arabia
Beijing	Hong Kong	Scotland
Belgium	India	Shanghai
Berlin	Ireland	Singapore
Bolivia	Italy	South Africa
Borneo	Jakarta	Spain
Brazil	Japan	Sri Lanka
Bulgaria	Korea	Sweden
Cambodia	Laos	Switzerland
Canada	London	Syria
Chicago	Malaysia	Taiwan
Chile	Mauritius	Thailand
China	Morocco	Tokyo
Costa Rica	Munich	Travel Safe
Cuba	Myanmar	Turkey
Czech Republic	Netherlands	United Arab
Denmark	New Zealand	Emirates
Ecuador	Pakistan	USA
Egypt	Paris	Vancouver
Finland	Philippines	Venezuela

For more information about any of these titles, please contact any of our Marshall Cavendish offices around the world (listed on page ii) or visit our website at:

www.marshallcavendish.com/genref